Praise for *Shannen and the Dream for a School*

"Janet Wilson has written a powerful account of the
true story of one Aboriginal girl's fight for safe and
comfortable schools for all children." —*CM Magazine*

"Both informative and politically rousing."
—*The Toronto Star*

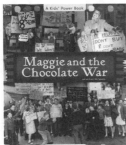

Praise for *Maggie and the Chocolate War*

"A great introduction to critical thinking and political
activism for young readers."
—*Canadian Bookseller*

"Highly recommended."
—*Children's Bookwatch: The MidWest Book Review*

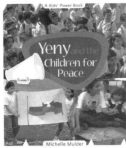

Praise for *Yeny and the Children for Peace*

"Tells the story of young Yeny and her protests against
Colombia's history of violent acts."
—*Children's Bookwatch: The MidWest Book Review*

"Tough to put down." —*CM Magazine*

Praise for *Lacey and the African Grandmothers*

"Lacey realizes that the African grandmothers remind
her of the elders in her own community."
—*Library of Clean Reads*

"Recommended." —*CM Magazine*

A Kids' Power Book

Severn
and the Day
She Silenced
the World

Janet Wilson

Second Story Press

Library and Archives Canada Cataloguing in Publication

Wilson, Janet, 1952-, author
Severn and the day she silenced the world / by Janet Wilson.

(The kids' power series)
For ages 9-13.
Issued in print and electronic formats.

ISBN 978-1-927583-23-4 (pbk.). —ISBN 978-1-927583-24-1 (epub)

1. Suzuki, Severn—Juvenile literature. 2. Child environmentalists—
Canada—Biography—Juvenile literature. 3. United Nations Conference
on Environment and Development (1992 : Rio de Janeiro, Brazil)—
Juvenile literature. I. Title. II. Series: Kids' power series

TD171.7.W54 2014   j363.7'0525092   C2014-900018-9

C2014-900019-7

Copyright © 2014 by Janet Wilson

Edited by Kelly Jones
Designed by Melissa Kaita
Icons © iStockphoto

Printed and bound in Canada

*Second Story Press gratefully acknowledges the support of the Ontario Arts Council
and the Canada Council for the Arts for our publishing program. We acknowledge the
financial support of the Government of Canada through the Canada Book Fund.*

Published by
Second Story Press
20 Maud Street, Suite 401
Toronto, ON M5V 2M5
www.secondstorypress.ca

Contents

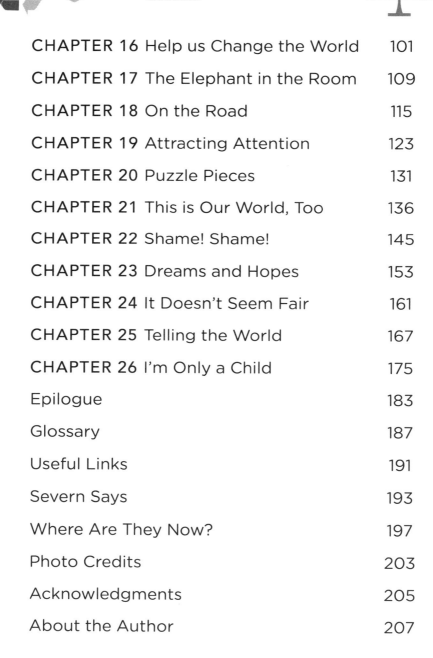

"In my anger, I am not blind, and in my fear, I am not afraid of telling the world how I feel."

Severn Cullis-Suzuki, June 12, 1992,

UN Earth Summit, Rio de Janeiro, Brazil

This book is dedicated to environmental activists David Suzuki and Tara Cullis. Thank you for your tireless and dogged devotion to raising awareness of the serious environmental problems facing humanity and our beautiful planet.

And to our dear friends Charles Simon, Anna Simon, John Cripton, and Linda Sword, for their valiant efforts toward our own community grassroots initiative, Eden Mills Going Carbon Neutral.

Author's Note

"To make a difference, you have to follow your heart."

Severn Cullis-Suzuki

The book you are about to read is based on a true story. All the characters are real, but parts of my telling of the tale are fiction. Often the people I interviewed could not clearly remember what was said or the order of events that took place more than twenty years ago, so I have woven into their memories information from videos, Environmental Children's Organization newsletters, books, articles, and a very special diary. I imagined most of the dialogue, but the excerpts from speeches appear as they were written. They are abbreviated, but Severn's speech to the United Nations Earth Summit is included in full. I appreciate everyone's contribution to this process, and their help and trust in me to recreate this inspiring story of young people telling the world how they feel about the most important issues of justice toward people, the planet, and their future.

Severn cuddles a woolly monkey from the Brazilian rainforest.

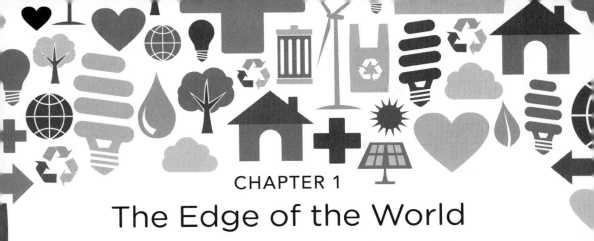

CHAPTER 1

The Edge of the World

"I'm involved in environmental issues because I love Nature and consider it part of me and me part of it."

Severn Cullis-Suzuki

March 1989

I *feel like I'm at the edge of the world.* Severn took a deep breath of salt air. She scanned the whole cove—the cliffs that dropped steeply into the Pacific Ocean and the forest-covered islets fading into the horizon from green to blue to mauve. A pair of eagles soared and swooped, scooping up fish discarded by fishing boats. Severn hugged her knees and squinted, searching the channel for porpoises. This was her favorite place on Earth.

I'm glad the tide is out, she thought, eyeing the beach, eager to discover the treasures left behind by the ocean waves. "C'mon, Sarika," she called, impatiently. When her sister and their two friends ran from the cabin, Severn followed them down the trail.

Oe (pronounced Oh-eh) and Tania walked boldly into the icy cold waves lapping at the edge of the beach. Severn couldn't believe it. They came from a tropical climate, after all.

The girls peered into a shallow tide pool. Severn pointed out sand dollars, barnacles, and tiny shore crabs darting in and out of seaweed. She popped a piece of bright green sea lettuce into her mouth. "Want some?"

Oe and Tania pulled 'No!' faces.

"This is a sea urchin," said Sarika, tickling the creature's spiky tentacles. Sarika was only five years old, but she was already an expert at identifying the inhabitants of the tide pools.

"Hey, I see starfish," Severn said, pointing to orange and purple sea stars flopped on their backs like lazy children, all arms and legs.

"Me, too!" Sarika cried.

"Good job, Little-Me-Too," said her father. He had walked from the cabin with Oe and Tania's parents.

Severn wanted to explain the most interesting fact about starfish—if you cut off an arm, another grows back—but she didn't know how to say that in the Kayapo language, and Oe and Tania only knew a few English words.

Oe's younger sister, Tania, reached for the starfish. "I have."

"Careful." As Severn placed the wiggling creature in her hands, she noticed that the black stripes of dye on Tania's arms had faded. Her hair was growing in, too. When the family arrived from Brazil two weeks earlier, Severn had tried not to stare at the shaved triangle above the girls' foreheads; now they had great punk rock hairdos.

Severn was prepared for the unusual appearance of their guests. She had been studying photos of the Kayapo people in their remote village in the Amazon rainforest. Colorful beaded strands hung from holes in their ear lobes and beads decorated their arms, necks, and legs. "Why don't they wear clothes?" she had asked her father as they looked at the photos.

"The patterns painted on their bodies are their clothes," he explained.

"But, Daddy, they'll get cold in Canada," Sarika said.

A more accurate name for starfish is sea stars, since they are carnivorous marine animals, not fish.

Sea urchins are also known as a sea hedgehogs.

5

"We'll have to find them clothes," said their mother, Tara, "and everything else the family will need. They'll be living in the apartment downstairs until it's safe to return home."

Imagine—a family from the Amazon rainforest coming to live with us in Vancouver, Severn had thought at the time. And now, here they were, having fun on the beach, and it didn't seem strange at all.

Severn had studied photos of the Kayapo before Oe and Tania arrived. These girls were dressed for a celebration.

"Hey, Dad." Severn pointed to a stream of water that spurted from the sand like a fountain. "A gooey-duck." She ran to the spot and started digging. "I can't get it out. It's pulling my hand down!"

Her father sprinted over to help. "You're not kidding, Sev. This one's really strong." Severn loved how her dad became so excited with anything to do with the natural world—just like a big kid. He pulled out a clam the size of a cereal bowl. "Wow, this one must be really old—it's huge!"

"Are we going to keep it?" Severn's family often collected food from the beach—oysters, littleneck clams, even shore crabs.

"Let's put this back just as we found it, sweetheart. Too many of these large clams are harvested." Severn knew the sadness in his voice meant he was thinking of all the marine life that was disappearing from the bay. Neighbors talked of a time when the waters were filled with abalone, red snapper, and cod as long as your arm. They remembered hearing schools of salmon slapping the water from miles away. Now, most of that is gone. That made Severn sad, too. Even though she was only nine years old, her heart told her this was wrong.

Severn and Sarika loved to catch fish, and eat them, too.
But now the fish were disappearing.

Sarika ran to a smaller spurt of water and began scooping out sand with a shell. She pulled out a smooth cookie-sized clam and rubbed her tummy to show their visitors it was delicious. Playing with Oe and Tania was like a marathon game of charades.

"Clam digging," Tara explained in Portuguese to the girls' father. Paiakan (pronounced Pie-ah-kahn) understood Portuguese, the language of Brazil, but his wife, Irekran, only spoke their Kayapo language. Baby Majal wasn't talking in any language yet. Soon everyone was digging for clams.

Severn's father, David, pried open a shell with his pocket knife. Paiakan screwed up his nose at the slimy blob inside. When David sliced off the clam and swallowed it whole, Irekran looked horrified.

Paiakan lost his enthusiasm for digging for clams, so he and Irekran (pronounced Eye-reh-krahn) returned to the cabin. Severn wondered why they sat on the deck with their backs facing the ocean. Were they homesick for their tropical forest? She knew what it felt like to miss the calm of forests. Severn loved their home back in Vancouver, a six-hour journey away by car, but after a few weeks of city life, she longed to return here to Quadra Island to explore, fish, and walk among the trees.

When the tide began to move in, Severn led the girls through the woods to play until the sun threw gold darts through the trees and the smell of cedar smoke drew them to the cabin. Oe and Tania joined their parents basking in the warmth of the fireplace. Severn had not seen the family so relaxed since they had fled Brazil.

Tonight, Paiakan did not seem like a man whose life was in serious danger.

Quadra Island is one of the Discovery Islands off the eastern coast of Vancouver Island in British Columbia, Canada.

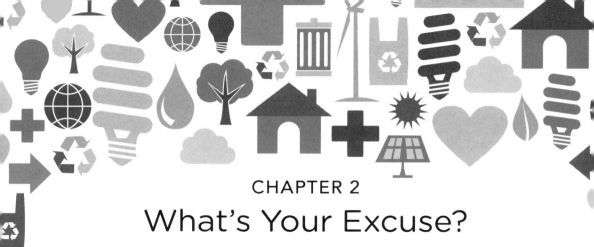

CHAPTER 2

What's Your Excuse?

"It is an awesome thing to know that you stand for something and that you will make a difference in the world."

Severn Cullis-Suzuki

"Mommy," Severn whispered so the younger girls playing dress-up didn't hear. "Tania pooed in the garden."

"Oh well," Tara said. "She's only four and in a completely new world." Severn's mother was in the kitchen of their Vancouver home preparing dinner.

"We should be happy—she's fertilizing our flowers." David wore a cheeky grin. Sometimes Severn couldn't tell if her dad was serious or pulling her leg. "Just think about how much perfectly useful, environmentally friendly human waste we flush down the toilet every day—and we use clean water to do it!" David was the host of a television science show called *The Nature of Things,* so he talked about the environment a lot. He had met Paiakan a couple of years earlier while filming a documentary about the destruction of the Amazon rainforest.

Severn had watched the program and learned that the Brazilian government cut down trees and gave the cleared rainforest land to unemployed city people so they could become farmers. The government called their campaign land with no people for people with no land. But indigenous people had lived on this "land with no people" for thousands of years. And what's more, the farms failed when the soil became infertile. Her father called it madness. "The Amazon rainforest is a treasure trove of plants and wildlife facing extinction."

It was natural that Severn shared her parents' passion for protecting forests—the lungs of Earth. When she was Sarika's age, Severn had heard that a forested area near her home was in danger of being logged. Even then she knew that trees help regulate the temperature and climate, and that destroying forests contributes to climate change. She had sold lemonade on her driveway to raise money to "Save the Stein Valley." She'd also sold her father's books for twenty-five cents. Later she'd found out they were worth a hundred times more than that!

"We tirsty," announced Oe, bursting through the door wearing Sarika's sparkly tiara. Severn smiled to hear Oe speak English. Before they had arrived, Severn wondered how they

Oe (left), Sarika, and Tania (right) play dress-up in the shower.

would converse with their guests. A friend of Tara's had taught them a few phrases in Portuguese, but there had been no need to worry. Through games and songs, the girls communicated beautifully. Oe and Tania were adventurous and enjoyed new experiences. They loved pedaling Sarika's tricycle around the neighborhood, watching television, and tobogganing down the mountain. Paiakan wanted no part of snow. He didn't like sight-seeing downtown, either. When he saw the tall buildings and stores filled with merchandise, he said, "To think that all this comes from the Earth. How long can it go on?"

"When do Oe and Tania have to go home?" Severn asked.

"They will return when Paiakan feels it is safe," Tara answered. The Kayapo chief had received death threats for leading an international protest that stopped the building of a series of large hydroelectric dams in Brazil's rainforest. This prevented the flooding of hundreds of villages and saved countless species of wildlife. Severn's parents were trying to raise money to buy a plane for Paiakan so he could escape if he was in danger. "Paiakan made many enemies in the government and big corporations—people who were going to make a lot of money building those dams." Severn's parents had worked with Paiakan for months to make the protest happen. She was proud that her mom and dad stood up for something they believed in; that they made a difference in the world.

"Why do adults care so much about money?" Severn muttered. "Nature is more important than money!" One-third of the Amazon had already been destroyed. *Will there be any rainforests left for my children to see?* she wondered.

The following week, the families flew north to meet First Nation communities who were also trying to protect their land and waters. The people of the longhouses felt a bond with Paiakan

Severn loved Haida culture, especially the drumming, singing, and dancing.

and many gave generously to help the Kayapo. One elder wearing a traditional woven cedar hat told Paiakan, "The terrible thing that is happening to you, we had that happen to us too."

The two families ended their trip on Haida Gwaii. Severn remembered visiting the islands a few years before, when her family had joined a battle to prevent the logging of magnificent old-growth forests. Severn loved the rich culture of the Haida and was deeply stirred by their ceremonies. She especially admired how they honored Earth and all its sacred gifts. When her class began studying First Nations in school, Severn had complained

Severn's family had protested the logging of
old-growth trees on the islands of Gwaii Haanas.

to her mother, "We only learn about past history. Some kids don't even know Aboriginal people are still living today." Severn was proud that her mom then took action and figured out a way to improve the curriculum.

On the way home from Haida Gwaii, Severn pressed her forehead to the plane window, glowering at the bald patches of forest that had been clear-cut and burned. Paiakan spoke to her mother in a grave voice. She translated his words for Severn: "In Brazil, forests are destroyed because people are poor and ignorant. Canadians are educated and rich. What's your excuse?"

Carved Haida poles are monuments to
commemorate ancestry, histories, people, or events.

CHAPTER 3
Best Show-and-Tell Ever

"Children are closer to creation. They haven't let go of the connection and love of Nature with all of its puddles, tadpoles, flowers, and furry creatures. They are part of Nature still."

Tara Cullis

"I have a great idea," Sarika said at breakfast. "Can Oe and Tania come to school with me for Show-and-Tell?"

Severn smiled. "That would be awesome, Sari."

David was standing at the counter making salmon sandwiches for their lunches. "I suppose that would be fine, *if* your teacher and Oe and Tania's parents approve."

"Maybe your dad will let you take the headdress Paiakan gave him—the one his mother made him," Tara said.

Her father's voice rose in panic. "But, Tara, that's one of my most prized possessions."

Paiakan wore one of his ceremonial chief headdresses.

"You don't have to worry, David. If we all go, Paiakan will take care of it."

A couple of days later, the Kayapo family stood in front of Sarika's kindergarten class. Paiakan explained that the bright yellow parrot feathers in the headdress represented the rays of the sun. Irekran showed the woven sling she used to carry baby Majal (pronounced Mah-yaal).

Questions came shyly at first. "What animals live in the Amazon?" "What do you eat?"

"Fruit and nuts are picked every day." Tara explained that there were no grocery stores. "The women harvest sugar cane, maize, and a kind of yam called manioc in village gardens. Men catch fish and hunt monkeys, tapir, and deer."

"Monkeys?" The children gasped.

"And big turtles," Sarika added.

"Do you watch television in your village?"

"You can't watch TV without electricity," said Sarika, rolling her eyes.

"What games do you play?"

The Kayapo girls giggled and kicked their feet.

"Soccer," the kids guessed, surprised they had something in common.

Later, Sarika boasted to Severn and Severn's friend Tove, "That was my best Show-and-Tell ever!"

"You and Severn always have the coolest stuff to show," said Tove. She and Severn were sketching some seashells they had found on the beach.

"Yeah, we're lucky to have a dad with a science program. He brings home the most amazing things," Severn replied.

Sometimes Severn wondered if her classmates thought she received special treatment because of her celebrity father. She had been on television, too—*Sesame Street* and her father's show. Her parents' interests had led the family to many places, including developing countries where Severn had seen how poor people live. Sometimes she wondered if kids in her school had any idea of how lucky they were. They never had to worry about having enough food, clean water, or a place to live.

"Do our other friends think I'm too serious because I'm always talking about Nature and people's rights?" Severn put down her pencil. "Did they think I was weird to have a beach clean-up birthday party?"

"Weird? Yes! But that's why we're your friends, Sev. You are never a bore."

"Well, I was named after a bore, you know," Severn said, grinning. "There's this river in England—the Severn—and it has the second largest tidal range in the world. It's a rare natural phenomenon called the Severn Bore."

"No way! We've been best friends since second grade and all this time I could have been calling you the Bore?" Tove laughed.

"Oh, my parents love to call me that. But I'd rather be called a rare natural phenomenon."

"Your parents are so cool. I learn more about science during dinners at your house than I do at school."

Dinner table discussions at Severn's house were pretty lively. Often they were about pollution, climate change, overpopulation, or holes in the ozone. Sometimes the conversations became pretty heated, especially when David despaired about the way people ignored environmental crises, or worse, denied them. "Changing people's attitudes is hopeless!" he had exclaimed one night.

"People can change, David." Tara was more optimistic. "We have to believe there is hope."

Severn wanted to believe that, too. But sometimes when she

heard her parents talk about the environment, she couldn't help but worry. If they didn't have solutions, what hope was there for her future? Sometimes Severn wished she wasn't so aware of Earth's problems. Was it normal for a nine-year-old to be so serious? Other kids' biggest worries seemed to be passing a math test or wearing the right brand of shoes.

But Severn felt fortunate to have parents who shared their love of the natural world, who encouraged her to catch butterflies, search ponds for frogs, play in tall grasses, and climb trees. Many of Severn's city friends hardly ever experienced the natural world. If they didn't know and love Nature, really love Nature,

The Kayapo family, Irekran, Majal, Tania, Paiakan, and Oe were grateful to be safe in Canada, but they missed their home in the rainforest.

Severn, Oe, Tania, and Sarika spent time playing in their backyard tree house.

why would they want to work to protect it?

After several weeks with the Suzuki family, Irekran told Paiakan she wanted to go home. "It's cold here. I miss my family. Our children should be in Aucre (pronounced Ah-oh-kray), going to school."

"Do you feel it is safe to return?" David asked.

Paiakan nodded. "Now that you have provided a plane for us, I can escape if there is danger." Finally, the Suzukis had raised enough money to buy a small plane for Paiakan.

On the day of their departure, Severn was startled when Irekran began a high-pitched, screeching wail. Tears flowed down her cheeks. Severn and Sarika burst into tears, too, realizing they might never see their friends again.

"Now, we must return what you have done for us," Paiakan said. "You must come and visit our home."

Severn and Sarika looked at each other, eyes wide open. "Daddy, can we go?" They pleaded in unison. "Mommy, please!"

"Well, I'd love for you to experience Aucre. It certainly was a life-changing trip for me." David's face lit up with a wide grin. "We could spend our summer vacation in the Amazon."

Tara leaned into her husband and the girls hugged them both.

CHAPTER 4
Back in Time

"The world is an incredible and beautiful place and will
be as long as we don't take it for granted."

Severn Cullis-Suzuki

"This doesn't look like the jungle," Sarika said, rubbing her eyes as they collected their bags at the Brazilian airport. They had arrived in the city of Manaus after a long journey that crossed many time zones.

"It's a jungle, all right," her dad muttered, holding onto Sarika tightly so she wouldn't be swept away by the current of travelers. "We still have a long way to go, sweetheart."

Severn clung to her mother, terrified she might be separated. Busy airports always made her anxious, just like her dad.

Two days later, they met Paiakan in Rendenção, a small and shabby town. Paiakan introduced the pilot and soon they were flying to Aucre. The trees seemed to roll below them like ocean waves. "It's like a beautiful green sea," Severn shouted over the noise of the plane.

"I think it looks like broccoli," yelled Sarika.

A few minutes later, the expanse of green was broken by a slash of red earth and foamy, cream-colored river. Severn asked, "What's that, Dad?"

"It's probably where there's a glacier gold mine—most likely an illegal one. Paiakan once led a band of warriors on a siege of an illegal gold mine in his territory. But the river was already polluted with mercury poison."

"It looks disgusting," Severn said.

After a couple of hours, the forest canopy parted to reveal a circle of red earth. Severn's eyes locked on an oval ring of huts near a river. "There's the village."

"And the Rio Zinho," said Tara. "It means little river."

Severn's stomach lurched as the plane lowered and bounced along a narrow landing strip among the trees. When the plane stopped, she heard shrill, high-pitched wails—the same kind of cries Irekran had made when she was leaving Canada.

"It's a Kayapo custom to cry to let people know they were missed," her father explained, as dozens of villagers ran to greet them.

Severn and Sarika stepped down the ladder into a crowd

of bodies painted black with red smeared faces, pungent with sweat. The women wore cotton dresses and the men wore shorts. The naked children pushed their way closer to Severn and Sarika, reaching eagerly to touch them.

"Oe! Tania!" Severn and Sarika spotted their friends in the crowd.

The sun seared Severn's bare skin before Paiakan led them to their hut. "Whew, it's cooler inside," she said. The mud-plastered walls and packed dirt floor dusted everything in red. The village children followed the family in, curious of every move.

A woman handed David four cloth hammocks. He scratched his head. "I have no clue how to hang these up." The villagers

Severn, Sarika, Oe, and Tania are happily reunited in Aucre.

laughed as if to say, "How is it possible for anyone to be so stupid?"

"Majal is getting big." Severn scooped up the toddler at Paiakan's hut next door after the family had organized themselves. Irekran was cooking beans, rice, and fish in metal pots over an open fire. She piled food high on tin plates. When they finished eating, Oe and Tania pulled the girls and their parents toward a path that led to the river. Oe and Tania charged right in. Severn's eyes asked her parents, can we go in, too? They nodded.

"Holy cow! It's like a bath." Even though the water was warm, Severn swooned with relief from the air's fiery heat. She floated lazily, watching the women and girls on the shaded banks throwing out baited hooks. Her father was interested to see what they were catching.

Kayapo villages are built in a circle to
reflect the Kayapo belief in a round universe.

"Guess what," he said pointing to a fish. "It's a piranha!"

Tara gasped. Piranhas have very sharp teeth and sometimes attack people, but Paiakan assured them the piranhas weren't a problem. He smacked his lips to say they were delicious.

Now and then, the women cooled themselves in the pool, or slapped their cupped hands in the water while chanting a song. Children collected clear water in pails from a depression where the water seeped out of the riverbank.

"That's their drinking water," David said. "The Kayapo were completely untouched by the modern world until about thirty years ago. This is the way they have lived for thousands of years."

It's like we're time-travelers, Severn thought.

"This life is idyllic." Tara slipped her arm through her husband's. "It's overwhelming."

Overwhelmed. That's how Severn felt, too.

After a while, Severn was curious to see the rest of the village. As she and Sarika climbed onto the bank, a throng of children trailed behind. They walked around the village stealing glances inside huts at people lying in hammocks or doing chores. "Sari, look. That girl is being painted." She nodded in the direction of a woman with black-dyed hands cradling a child.

Severn had been meaning to ask her father an important question. "Pops, I have to pee. Where do I go?"

Her father gestured toward an outhouse made of woven grass screens. Inside was an open pit. "You put a foot on either side, then squat, just like when we camp," David said. Then he warned, "But, be sure not to look down."

"Oh, gross!" Severn gasped at a mass of writhing fat maggots below.

Her dad laughed. "I told you not to look."

In the center of the village, several men were gathered under a canopy, chatting and smoking carved pipes. "Paiakan said this is the men's hut," Tara said.

Sarika leaned in to see what they were making. "They're weaving slings like the one Irekran used to carry Majal."

"Why do some men have a hole below their mouth, Dad?" asked Severn.

"They are for labrets—a traditional adornment." He explained that large wooden disks are inserted into the lower lip. "Most of the younger men choose not to follow this custom."

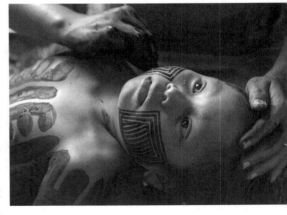

Severn and Sarika watched a girl being painted with black dye from the genipap tree.

"I'm not surprised," Severn said. "It must be uncomfortable."

Later, the family was invited to a welcome feast the women had prepared. A huge hunted turtle was plunked on its back in the fire. David had eaten turtle when he was a boy, but this didn't seem very appetizing, especially the skin, all goose-bumpy and wrinkled. Paiakan ripped off a bloody leg and gave it to him. Severn knew her father would eat it to be polite. She was curious to taste the turtle, but not until it cooked a little longer.

When Sarika fell asleep on her dad's shoulder, he said, "We should all go to bed. Tomorrow Paiakan is taking us down the river to fish." Severn was thrilled; like their dad, she and Sarika adored fishing.

"I wish Grampa was with us," Severn said, snug in her hammock. Their grandfather had taken the girls fishing ever since they had been able to hang on to a fishing line. They used to fish around Vancouver—until they caught fish with tumors. Now they only fished away from the city.

Severn thought about the polluted river she'd seen from the plane. Could the fish die and disappear from the River Zinho? Being so remote it hardly seemed possible. If the river was in danger, she would want to fight to protect it, just like her parents. Lulled by the steady chirping of cicadas, Severn's eyelids grew heavy, then closed.

CHAPTER 5

Fishing on the River Zinho

"Why not think of disposables as unacceptable and try to avoid disposable things if possible?"

Severn Cullis-Suzuki

"Sev," Sarika whispered from her hammock. Fingers of morning light streamed through the opening of the hut. "They're staring at us!"

Severn opened her eyes. Inches away, a row of children's eyes watched them patiently. More villagers idled around the walls of the hut.

"It's like we're their morning cartoons," said Tara. "I guess it's time to get up."

After a breakfast of bananas and guavas with leftovers, the sisters ran to the river to watch the men prepare their dug-out canoes for the fishing expedition. The girls' mother was talking to Paiakan nearby. As she turned and walked toward them, her lips were clamped in a frown. "I'm afraid we can't go."

"Why not?" Severn stomped her foot into the red dirt. "Because we're kids?"

"That's not fair," Sarika said, stomping, too. "That boy is going and he's little like me."

"He can go *because* he's a boy." Her mother stroked Sarika's ponytail. "Paiakan said, 'No females allowed.'"

Sarika had never heard of such a rule.

"You're kidding, right?" Severn knew she wasn't.

"Kayapo males and females have very different roles. The men hunt and fish while the women garden, make meals, and care for the children." Her mother's voice brightened. "Daddy will explain to Paiakan that in our culture males and females participate in the same activities."

The girls walked back to the clearing where they joined some children playing soccer. When the heat became unbearable, they played toss the giant lemon in the river. By the time their father returned from fishing, his daughters had almost forgotten their disappointment.

"See what I caught!" Their father held up a huge fish. "The others scoffed at my collapsible fishing rod, but I said, 'This is good strong line.' Every time it broke, they roared with laughter." David laughed at himself, too. "I hooked the tucunaré and played him to exhaustion like my father taught me. Then my rod snapped in two. I pulled on the line and then *wham*, an arrow impaled the fish. I turned around and there was Paiakan with a bow and arrow."

Severn said, "So Paiakan caught the fish."

"No way! *I* caught the fish. The chief might have killed it." The Kayapo didn't need to understand the words to join in the laughter.

Villagers have learned to play soccer since they have had more contact with people outside their own culture.

The next day, the girls got their wish and all the visitors set out on another fishing expedition. The River Zinho twisted and turned, sometimes narrowing into a swiftly flowing channel, then widening into a long deep pool or becoming shallow with deep riffles.

"I see a toucan." Severn pointed to the trees hanging over the shore.

"Me too," Sarika shouted. "And Daddy, look. Giant hamsters!"

"Capybaras—the world's largest rodent."

When they reached a wide, shallow area, Paiakan climbed

A fully grown capybara may reach a length of over 4 ft (130 cm) and weigh more than 140 lbs (65 kg).

out of the boat and walked across the rocks, staring down. He pulled back his bow and shot an arrow. When the prey stopped slapping about, Paiakan lifted a long, snake-like creature from the water.

"An electric eel." David was beaming. Then his smile vanished. This eel could deliver a shock that could be fatal to a small child. Paiakan made sure it was dead before he put it in the bottom of the canoe. Still, Severn was nervous with an electric eel under her feet.

When they returned, the women met the canoes to admire

Paiakan (right) lifted the electric eel he had caught into the canoe on a fishing expedition.

the fish and congratulate Paiakan on his eel. At dinner, Severn was curious to taste the catch of the day, especially the eel.

"This type of eel is a highly prized delicacy—it is only for the elders," her father said.

"Rats," said Severn, under her breath.

For the rest of the evening, Paiakan recounted David's clumsy attempts at fishing until everyone was laughing.

"Time for bed," said her father, pretending to be insulted.

"But it's just starting to get dark," whined Sarika.

"In Aucre we go to bed when the sun goes down and wake up when it rises."

When Severn slipped into her hammock, she had the urge to reach for a book, then remembered—no lights. It was the first time she had missed electricity. She hadn't even thought about phones, televisions and radios, or computers. She didn't miss her other possessions, either—her sports equipment, art supplies, music. Looking around the hut, Severn was struck again by how few things there were. Her house in Vancouver was cluttered with stuff. Here, most of the things the Kayapo used decomposed naturally. The only pieces of garbage she'd seen since arriving were the packages of fruit drinks and soup her mother had brought. *We buy and throw away so much!* Severn remembered what Paiakan had said. "To think that all this comes from the earth. How long can it go on?"

Today, the Kayapo use more and more modern
materials, like plastic, that cannot decompose.

Onça-Pintada!

"I am trying to save the knowledge that the forests and this planet are alive, to give it back to you who have lost the understanding."

Paulinho Paiakan, Kayapo chief

"Stay close at *all* times," their mother warned, looking directly into her daughters' eyes. "The rainforest is not like the forests at home. There are many, many dangers."

"We know, Mommy." Severn tried to sound brave, but as they walked she told herself, *don't you dare get lost.*

At the edge of the forest, they met the villagers who would be their guides and followed them slowly through a warm and wet mist. It was dim, like twilight, broken here and there by angled shafts of light.

Paiakan pointed out the different trees bearing nuts and fruits along the way. David said, "The Kayapo know a lot about the medicinal powers of jungle plants. About a third of our modern medicines come from the rainforest. Isn't that amazing?"

Suddenly, Severn's heart almost stopped. She grabbed her father. "Daddy, we lost the guides!"

"Don't worry, sweetheart." David held her close, pointing to the trail ahead. "They're right there. The dark patterns on their bodies are like camouflage."

Sure enough, when Severn squinted, the guides came into focus.

"Hey, look at this gigantic ant!" Sarika cried. She knew her dad was crazy about any kind of insect.

"Wow! You have such eagle eyes for finding interesting specimens," her father said, patting his daughter on the back.

Severn was giddy with the intensity of the jungle—the mingling of a musky decay smell with sweet, fragrant flowers and fresh oxygen; the saturated brilliant colors of electric blue macaws, lipstick-pink orchids, iridescent yellow butterflies; and the wildest sounds imaginable from squawking birds and screeching monkeys. Every time she heard a howl, Severn looked up only to see the rustling of leaves. It was magical! How would she ever be able to describe this experience to Tove?

The next day, the family went on a fishing expedition in the opposite direction. After paddling for an hour, they beached the canoes on sandbars. Paiakan followed finger-sized trails in the sand to where they ended, dropped to his knees, and began digging until he found a small round egg.

"Turtles!" Severn exclaimed. She searched for trails and began scooping out handfuls of sand. "I found one over here."

"Me, too," Sarika shouted.

"*Onça-pintada*!" Severn halted at the sound of Paiakan's voice. It was loud and sharp. Where were her parents? She and

The Amazon rainforest produces more than
twenty percent of the world's oxygen.

Sarika had been so busy digging, they hadn't noticed that they had wandered.

Then her parents called in alarm. "Severn, Sarika! Come back!" Severn sucked in air. "Sari, let's go." They ran to the canoes.

"*Tem onça-pintada.*" Paiakan pointed to the trees beyond the dunes. Severn had never seen him so worried.

Severn and Sarika lifted turtle eggs carefully
from nests, leaving some to hatch.

The jaguar is the largest cat found in the Americas. Its name means 'a beast that kills its prey with one leap.'

"Jaguars." Her mother covered her heart with her hands. Her father hustled the girls into the canoes.

"I'll be more careful not to wander away. I promise," Severn said shakily, searching the shadows in the bushes. "But wouldn't it be cool to see a jaguar?"

They drifted lazily with the current, until big, warm drops of rain began to plop down all around them. The canoes were banked and Paiakan ran toward the forest. It began to pour down so heavily Severn could hardly breathe. Paiakan ran back with giant banana leaves.

"Umbrellas!" Severn cried.

Once the tropical squall passed, everyone had a chance to fish. After someone caught a large tucunaré, they beached the canoes and lit a fire. Pieces of fish were placed on banana leaves, drizzled with fresh lemon and salt, then folded into packages and tossed into the fire.

"I'm starving," said Severn, as they pulled the wraps out. She opened a package and dug right in to her delicious steamed meal complete with its own disposable picnic plate.

The red-and-yellow sunset was spectacular, but as the forest grew inky black, Severn felt quivery in the pit of her stomach. Her father shone his flashlight at the shore as they maneuvered their canoes into the current.

"I see eyes!" Sarika scrambled onto her mother's lap.

"*Jacare*, they're everywhere," her father said spookily. Alligators! Severn dug fingers into his arm. She became even more alarmed when everyone had to get out to pull the canoes over some rocks. Finally, after many hours of traveling in the pitch dark, they came to the familiar bend in the river. Severn let out a huge sigh of relief.

Her heart didn't stop fluttering until she was snug in her hammock. All the incredible events of the day swirled around her brain. Now she understood why her parents spent so much time organizing international protests and raising money to help Paiakan fight the government and corporations to protect his way of life and home from being lost forever. Next time her mom and dad had to go away on a trip, she wouldn't feel so upset. Severn vowed to do her part to help save rainforests.

But what could she possibly do?

CHAPTER 7
Bad Omens

"We are now the most numerous mammal in the world, and with technology, consumption, and a global economy, we are undermining the very things that keep us alive and healthy."

David Suzuki

The next morning, Severn was eager to try the boiled turtle eggs. She popped one into her mouth. It tasted like chalk. Her first impulse was to spit it out, but that would insult her hosts. She swallowed and reached for a banana to get rid of the taste.

"Mommy, I have a sliver." Sarika held up her bare foot.

"David, get the first aid kit, please." Tara examined the small volcano erupting between Sarika's toes.

"Ouch!" Sarika yelped. Her mother poked an opening with a disinfected needle. She swabbed the sore clean and put on a bandage. "Wear your runners from now on, okay?"

"Okay." Sarika ran off to play with her friends.

"Hey Sev, have a look at what Mom took out of Sari's foot." Her father dangled a fat worm. Severn's mouth dropped. "It's a parasite that sheds eggs in the ground and burrows into mammals passing by." Severn hopped right over to get her runners, too.

"We're very lucky, Sev," her mother said, as women painted dark from head to foot came into the village center. "The tribe is beginning a three-day women's festival." For about an hour, the women chanted in unison and danced in rows facing the huts.

Sarika points out where the parasitic worm was in her foot.

The next day, women appeared wearing many strands of glass seed beads and feather headdresses. Oe and Tania were transformed by their paint and beads. Severn and Sarika watched, mesmerized, as they sang and danced.

On the third day of celebrations, the women donned even more spectacular adornments—large wooden frames supporting

Oe and Tania's aunt is dressed for the festival.

huge feather headdresses that towered above them. The dancing began before sundown and continued into the pitch-black night. But the magic of the festival was about to disappear.

The first sign of trouble was when the community found out that a woman, who had been airlifted to a hospital with serious injuries before their arrival, had died. Not long after, an old man died unexpectedly.

"A relative is sweeping away the spirits," her mother explained, as Severn watched someone sweep the grounds around the dead man's hut. Severn was shocked to see the man's feet sticking out of the doorway of his hut filled with mourners. It was the first time she'd seen a dead body. "What will they do with him, Dad?"

"The Kayapo leave their deceased on a platform to be consumed by the forest."

At first, Severn was surprised. Then she thought about her own culture—we burn dead bodies or bury them in the ground where they rot and get eaten by worms. The Kayapo way was pretty natural, too. *I guess no matter which culture we belong to, our bodies return to the Earth*, she thought.

A couple of days later, Severn awoke to shouting in the night. Then gunfire cracked through the cool air. Her parents left their hammocks and went to the door. Paiakan was standing outside their hut as if he were on guard.

"What's wrong?"

"The moon is sick," he said pointing to the full moon, "and my people are very frightened."

What does he mean, "the moon is sick"? wondered Severn. She joined her parents.

"Have a look," her father said. The full moon was huge, mottled brown and orange. As soon as they saw it, Severn and her parents knew it was a lunar eclipse.

"The people are chanting the moon back to health," Paiakan said. "They're blaming the *brancos*."

Severn knew that brancos were white people. Maybe the Kayapo figured that too much contact with their visitors had brought the tragedies—the deaths and now the eclipse.

Her mother drew Severn closer. "Do you think we're in danger?"

"*Não sei*," Paiakan said, gravely. I don't know.

"Do you think the villagers will calm down?" her mother asked.

"Não sei."

"David, I am worried." Tara turned and motioned her husband and daughter into the hut.

"I'm worried, too," David admitted. "If they feel we have brought bad omens, it's wise to leave as soon as possible. The Kayapo can be very fierce people."

Not knowing what else to do, the family went back to their hammocks. The shouting and gunshots continued as Severn tried to sleep. She curled up into a tight ball to keep from trembling, trying to make sense of all that had happened. The Kayapo had been friendly and she had felt at home here, so it was a shock to suddenly be reminded that they were outsiders— strangers from a modern world who in many ways represented the destruction of this natural world. For the first time, Severn felt very conflicted about her own culture and confused about being in Aucre. But mostly she was sad that their idyllic trip was coming to a crashing end.

CHAPTER 8

Smoke Signals

"The threat to my friends and to the animals made me feel angry and helpless. When I got back to Canada, I decided I had to help them."

Severn Cullis-Suzuki

" I don't want to go," Sarika sobbed.

"I know Sari, but a plane is coming for Paiakan and Irekran today. We've decided it is best to go with them."

Sarika cried louder. "No, it's best to stay!"

Severn felt like bawling, too. The commotion of the other night had ended. Today it seemed as if nothing had happened, but she felt an unfamiliar silence around the people.

"Let's get packing," her father said. "We need to lighten the load on the plane so let's leave behind anything we don't need."

As they walked to the plane, the young Kayapo crowded around the visitors to say good-bye. Her parents handed over

The dyes painted on the children usually last for ten days.

Ceremonial life is very important to the Kayapo
and continues throughout the year.

flashlights and fishing gear, mosquito nets, the first aid kit—anything that was useful. A young man who had been on the fishing trips, handed Severn a feather necklace he'd made.

"Thank you," Severn whispered, then dissolved into tears. Sarika sobbed again and soon everyone was crying. The villagers wept and wailed in the same way they had when the family first arrived.

Once they were on the plane, Severn asked her father, "Do you think the villagers were crying for the same reason we were crying? Because we're friends. Or because Paiakan is leaving?"

"I don't know, Sev. The Kayapo accepted us as friends and treated us well. But our world represents a threat to the survival of their culture, their home, and their way of life. Think about all the material possessions we gave away. The Kayapo are completely self-sufficient without these amenities. But when we come along and show them what they could have, their sense of themselves changes a little bit."

As they flew away, Severn thought about her dad's words. It was true—everything the Kayapo needed to survive was within reach. They didn't need money in Aucre. Severn had learned that the Kayapo word for money was "dirty paper." Yet in her world, money was so important. It seemed to make people happy. But the Kayapo seemed content without it....

Severn's thoughts were interrupted. In the distance, she

spotted a tall column of white smoke rising from the green forest.

"Mommy, look. Fire!" Severn knew about wildfires in British Columbia. They could do a lot of damage. Were her friends in Aucre in danger?

"I'm afraid they're not wildfires, sweetheart," her mother said, sadly. "They're deliberately set to clear land for farms."

Images of the rainforest she had explored—the birds, the butterflies and beetles, the magnificent old-growth trees, flowers, animals—flashed behind her eyes. It was all too much to imagine them being destroyed. *This is wrong!*

Scientists estimate that rainforest the size of a football field is being destroyed every second.

Then Severn saw another plume, and another, and another. She looked at Paiakan sitting in stony silence, his eyes narrowed and jaw clenched. *What was he was thinking? I know how I'd feel if this were my home,* Severn thought. *Very angry. Very sad.*

Soon the smoke became so thick it blocked the sun. It seeped into the plane. Sarika started to cry. Severn remembered her dad's documentary about the importance of trees and how their destruction changes the temperature of the planet. Severn knew all that. But as their plane flew over the smoke and flames, the reality hit hard. *This is where the Kayapo live—in the middle of this.*

When the plane landed, Rendenção seemed polluted and scruffy compared to Aucre. As they made their way to the motel, Severn noticed that the people here didn't seem as clean, happy, or well-nourished as her friends in Aucre. The family settled into their beds for the night, but Severn was still haunted by the smoke.

"What's the matter, Sev?" Her mother slipped in beside her. "Are you crying?"

"It's so stupid!" Severn snapped. "How can people deliberately burn down rainforests?"

Tara sighed. "I know. It seems crazy. But Brazilians are doing it out of desperation. The farmers are poor. They need to make a living for their families by clearing land for their farms."

"But what about the Kayapo?"

"Maybe people don't understand that their actions are hurtful to other people, and some are so prejudiced that they don't care."

"But how can it be allowed?" Severn was practically shouting. "Why does the government agree to this?"

Her mother didn't answer. It was clear that she didn't have the answer. Maybe no one did.

"It's been a long day, honey," Tara said, brushing wisps of hair from Severn's face. "Try to sleep. Think about all the good people and beautiful things in the world."

Severn managed a weak smile hoping to disguise how disturbed she really felt. She believed in her parents. They always seemed to have answers to her questions; they knew what to do. She wanted her mother to say, "Everything is going to be all right."

But could any parent really say that anymore?

Severn's parents had taught her that anyone can make a difference if they try. "You are what you do, not what you say," her dad always said. Severn knew her parents were working hard and trying their best to help save rainforests. But she wanted to do something, too. *I can't wait until I'm grown up to make a difference,* she said to herself. *I have to help now.*

But what could one ten-year-old girl do?

CHAPTER 9
The First Step

"Working in a group is a good way to be effective because you can support each other and make more of an impact than you can on your own."

Severn Cullis-Suzuki

"Oh Tove, Aucre is another world!" Severn said, breathlessly. The memories of her adventures cascaded out in a steady stream—piranhas, jaguars, turtle eggs, giant ants, parrots, mud huts and hammocks, bows and arrows, electric eels.

Tove sat cross-legged on the bed in Severn's room, painting every image in her mind, but there was so much to take in at once.

"And Sarika had a worm buried in her foot." Severn paused and exhaled. "But the most amazing part was exploring the rainforest. You must see a real jungle one day—if they haven't all been burned down!"

Tove was surprised at the sharp turn of Severn's voice. "What do you mean?"

Severn had planned to talk about all the best parts of her trip, but the worst part tumbled out too—the fires. "Tove, my heart broke. Once an old-growth rainforest is destroyed, it will never be the same." Severn's voice climbed. "And what about the animals that will lose their homes and become extinct, lost forever? And what will happen to the Kayapo?"

"Why are they burning forests? I don't get it."

"I don't either. It doesn't make any sense. My dad told me about a periwinkle plant that increased the chances of children surviving leukemia—eight out of ten kids are living instead of dying. Now it's extinct in the wild. If they burn down the forest, scientists will never discover other plants that might cure diseases like cancer."

A sloth cuddles her baby in the Children's Eternal Rainforest, Costa Rica.

"We kids wouldn't be so dumb if we were in charge," Tove muttered. "But we can't even vote."

Severn brightened. "You know what? Kids are making things happen. My dad is doing a show about the Monteverde Cloud Forest in Costa Rica." Severn detected a question behind Tove's eyes so she added, "Cloud forests are rainforests without as much pre-cipitation. A thirteen-year-old boy discovered a golden toad in that forest that no biologist had ever seen before. That made scientists excited to discover other hidden species."

"Wow, a kid discovered a new species. Cool!" Severn could always count on Tove to be impressed by stories about animals and plants.

"And a fifth-grade class in Sweden heard about the threats to the same forest so they raised money to buy up acres so that land could never be logged."

Costa Rica's Monteverde Cloud Forest
is one of the planet's most bio-diverse habitats.

"But how would kids have enough money to buy land?"

"They started by fundraising and when kids around the world heard about it, they raised more money to buy more land. Those acres became the Children's Eternal Rainforest. Kids are still sending in donations—kids in Canada, too. My dad says this shows young people really can have a big effect."

"Maybe we could raise money."

"Now you're talking. Maybe we could start a club to save the environment."

"That would be awesome." Tove fell back on the bed. "We could really do something if we worked together."

"And it would be way more fun."

"We could sell crafts at the school fair."

"And books." Severn winced at the memory of selling her father's books. "Used books." She spotted small plastic pieces of Fimo clay on a shelf behind Tove. The bright squares reminded her of the vivid colors she'd seen in the jungle. "I have an idea of what we can make."

In September, Severn started sixth grade at Lord Tennyson Elementary. It was always a challenge to start the new school year and speak in French again. She and Tove hung out with a circle of friends who were all bright and lively. They ran neck and neck for the best marks, but also for the best jokes. They loved to talk and make each other laugh, sometimes uncontrollably. At lunch, the girls met to catch up on their summer vacations.

Michelle noticed the green lizards with red spots pinned to Severn and Tove's T-shirts. "Those are adorable!"

"Geckos," Vanessa said, her eyebrows dancing. "Where'd you get them?" Severn explained that she and Tove made the pins from Fimo.

Morgan chuckled. "Love the sunglasses." Everything either made Morgan laugh or made her mad.

"Tove and I had this idea to sell crafts to raise money to save rainforests." While they ate, Severn talked about her trip. Then she described the fires.

"Rainforests are being destroyed in Colombia, too," Michelle told them. She had visited her mother's family in South America. "Mostly to raise cattle for fast-food restaurants."

"That makes me want to be a vegetarian," said Morgan, "except for the not-eating-hamburgers part."

Michelle started to giggle. "Don't make me laugh—this is serious!"

"Do you want help making geckos?" Vanessa asked. "We could have fun and help you save rainforests at the same time."

Tove and Severn exchanged smiles. Severn asked, "Would you join our environment club?"

"I'd love to," said Michelle. "There must be something kids can do to help the environment."

"Me, too." Vanessa pulled her chair closer. "What's the name of your club?"

Tove and Severn looked blank. "We don't have one yet."

"How about ECO?" Morgan's brain worked at lightning speed.

Severn scrunched her nose. "You mean like the sound—echo?"

"I mean the letters E-C-O, to stand for Environmental Children's Organization. Get it?"

The girls were impressed with Morgan's suggestion once they got it.

"Come to my house for our first ECO meeting," Severn said. "We'll make geckos."

For the first time since she saw the smoke, Severn felt lighter—more hopeful. Her parents were right. Taking action, even if it was small, felt better than complaining and feeling helpless. Severn was taking her first step on a journey. She had no idea where that step would lead or how many steps she'd take, but having good friends to share the adventure gave her courage. And hope.

CHAPTER 10
Stop Wrecking the Planet

"I think the most power you have as young people is the power of your heart—your desire to help the world and make a difference. As people get older, they lose that. So follow your passion!"

Severn Cullis-Suzuki

"I want to make geckos, too," Sarika pouted.

"Mommy, can you get Sari to do something else, please," Severn whispered to her mother as the ECO girls worked on their pins for the school craft fair. "She's too little to make geckos."

"All the better to make tiny spots with her teeny fingertips," Morgan cackled. She showed Sarika how to roll little balls.

"Sari could make better geckos than I can. Mine look terrible," Michelle groaned. "I'll never be as artistic as Severn and Tove."

"How much should we charge?" Vanessa asked.

"How 'bout a dollar?" Morgan asked.

"Mom suggested ten," said Severn. "She says people will pay more for a worthy cause."

Michelle and Morgan gasped. Ten dollars was a lot of money. "No one would pay that much."

"But these are handmade," said Tove. "People pay more for my dad's furniture because it's created by an artist. And don't forget the materials are expensive."

"The higher the price, the fewer geckos to make," Vanessa said.

Morgan jumped up again, throwing her hands in the air. "We'll call them, ECO-Geckos!"

"Hey, Sev. Is this some kind of lizard factory?" A tall, slim young man with a camera slung around his neck leaned over the table. "You know child labor violates your rights."

Severn chuckled and slapped his hand. She turned to her friends. "This is our friend Jeff Gibbs." Jeff founded the Environmental Youth Alliance, a network of youth activists from across Canada. He was still a student when he had protested against the mega-dams in Brazil and logging in British Columbia.

"It's very cool that you guys have formed an environment club," Jeff said, snapping a few photos. "I should introduce you to the gang at the EYA office. We'd be into helping you out."

The girls thanked him as he left the room. "You never told us about Jeff!" Morgan chirped. "He's cute."

"Nevermind. That cute guy's too old for you," Severn said. "Let's get on with our meeting. I'll take minutes." Tara had taught the girls how to record what they discussed. While making geckos, they also hatched plans to learn more about environmental problems.

"I'll design a sign for our craft table," said Tove, "and we should have flyers to inform people what ECO is all about."

"Great," Vanessa agreed. "But what is our most important message?"

Severn pressed her lips together and thought hard. "We need to tell the world how we feel about the way adults are treating the Earth. This is our world, too."

Jeff Gibbs sits in front of a clear-cut forest on Haida Gwaii.

"Yeah, they should start thinking about us for a change," said Morgan, fumbling with the gecko's sunglasses, "and stop wrecking the planet."

"We only have one!" Vanessa added. "And look at what a mess they're making."

"Grown-ups tell us kids to clean up our mess," Michelle grumbled, "then they go ahead and do the very thing they tell us not to do."

Jeff, Tara, Severn, and Sarika often
hiked in the forests of British Columbia.

"That's very kind of Jeff to offer to help," her mother said when Severn asked for permission to go to the EYA after school. "He'll be a wonderful mentor and teach you a lot about activism."

The next day, the girls walked up the steps of an old red-brick house near where Severn lived. Young people sat at computers and stood over large photocopy machines. Hip-hop blared on the radio. Jeff made a few introductions. "This is Doug Ragan—he runs the place."

Doug was a warm and smiley guy. "We believe raising awareness is very important." He handed out some magazines. "EYA has programs for educating youth about environmental issues and activism."

"Do you think we could write something like this?" Tove asked, leafing through an EYA publication.

"Sure we could," said Vanessa, who was always willing to try new things.

"We'll show you how to put together a newsletter and help print it," Doug said.

"Wow. You mean I could be a real journalist?" Morgan asked. "Fame and fortune, here I come."

"Speaking of fortune, how could we afford to print these?" Vanessa asked.

"No problem. We have some funds for youth outreach. I can also help you apply to a credit union that gives money to young people for environmental causes. In the meantime, start thinking about topics for ECO's first edition. I suggest you pick something that interests you."

"What about the hole in the ozone?" Michelle was intrigued by a poster, The Sunshine is our Right Campaign.

"Great idea. EYA is really into this issue. We're planning a beach walk to talk to suntanners about the dangers of ozone depletion. Did you know that people in Australia and New Zealand aren't allowed to be in the sun during certain times of the day?"

As he walked the girls to the door, Doug explained the issue in more detail. The girls listened with rapt attention pleased to be treated seriously and with respect. "When your articles are ready, we'll help you put the newsletter together."

"Thanks so much," Severn said. Doug's and Jeff's kindness was energizing.

In this moment, anything felt possible.

CHAPTER 11
Endangered People

"How can we tell poor countries how to treat their forests if we're doing the same damaging things here? Young people must question authority and join the efforts to save old-growth forests."

Jeff Gibbs

During the winter, Jeff invited the Suzukis to a benefit to help save the rainforests of Sarawak in Borneo, the largest island in Malaysia.

Severn had been incredibly moved by the two indigenous speakers who had left Borneo to tell the world about being pushed off their land by international corporations. Their stories of logging destroying their food source and polluting their water were similar to the First Nations people she had met in Canada, South America, and Australia. They were all fighting to protect their land and their way of life from being swallowed by the modern world. Severn couldn't imagine a world without the rich culture of peoples that had endured for centuries. Now she realized that just like endangered animals, entire cultures and groups of people could become extinct, too.

Her father must have read her thoughts. "It might not be safe for these two speakers to return to their families if the government finds out they're telling the truth about their fate to the rest of the world."

Severn thought about Paiakan, then remembered the polluted water in Brazil. "It's not fair. Rich countries have clean water. Shouldn't all people have the same right?"

"Clean water is a basic human right, but those rights are violated, especially in poor countries," Severn's mother said.

"Do you think ECO could help the people in Borneo?"

"Well, you know they have a critical need for clean water," her mother said. "What about raising money for a water filter?"

"What a great plan!" Severn liked the idea of buying something really useful with their donations. "I'm sure the girls will be into that."

"I call this ECO meeting to order," said Michelle, munching on one of the licorice sticks Doug provided for their meetings at EYA headquarters. "Severn, you have the first item on the agenda."

She told her friends all about the Penan people in Borneo and asked if they'd like to raise money for the water filter. "We could give them our donations when they pass through Vancouver in a couple of months."

The girls lit up. "Our first fundraiser!" Tove exclaimed.

"Let's make it a fun-raiser," quipped Morgan.

"All in favor, raise your licorice," said Michelle. Five hands went up. "Motion passed. Now, let's see your contributions to our first newsletter."

Jeff Gibbs presented Penan children in Borneo with a mural from Canadian children.

Tove and Severn passed around their cartoons.

"You guys are fantastic artists." Vanessa shook her head in amazement.

Michelle flattened out some typed pages. "I'll read what I have written so far.

"What are CFCs? During a regular day, you most likely open your fridge, turn on the air-conditioning, and then have a drink out of a Styrofoam cup. But did you know that all of these every-day things contain CFCs (chlorofluorocarbons)?"

The article explained that CFCs float up to the ozone layer, a shield that protects Earth's atmosphere from the sun's harmful ultraviolet rays. "They've eaten a hole in the ozone about the size of the Antarctic." Michelle slapped her hand on the table.

"If scientists know about this, why don't people just stop using CFCs?" Tove tapped her head. "Sounds like a no-brainer to me."

"The hole keeps growing every day and people act as if they have all the time in the world to fix it," Michelle grumbled, shaking her head.

"There are lots of things scientists don't know how to do," Vanessa said. "Like bringing back an animal that's gone extinct."

"And they don't know how to bring life back to a desert," Tove said.

"Why are people allowed to break things they don't know

how to fix?" Morgan was practically shrieking. "And they don't even get into trouble for doing it!"

"Kids sure would!" Severn could feel her pulse thumping. She changed the subject to the next order of business on the agenda. "Madame Robichaud asked about my gecko so I told her all about ECO. She asked if we would make a presentation about rainforests to the school."

The girls blurted an excited, "Yes!" All except Tove. "I'm not so sure that I want to speak in front of the whole school." She fingered strands of her blonde hair. "I'd be a nervous wreck."

"But you'll be fine if we present together." Severn smiled at her friend with encouraging eyes. Tove was the shyest member of their group. "Oh, and remind me to ask my folks if we can borrow their projector and some slides. They have lots of books for our research, too."

The following week, the ECO members sat in chairs at the front of the gymnasium as four hundred students filed in. The principal addressed the audience about the importance of the environment to their school. "That's why you have blue boxes in all your classrooms."

Vanessa started by telling the students all about ECO. Next

up was Michelle who talked about the importance of rainforests in maintaining the water cycle around the world. When it was Morgan's turn, she held her fingers up in a peace sign and pumped her fist in the air. "I'd like to thank the members of the Academy for my Oscar—oops wrong speech!" When the laughter finished traveling around the room, she spoke about acid rain and the ozone layer.

When Tove spoke at the microphone, her ECO friends encouraged her silently knowing how much courage it took for her to stand there. Her voice was soft as she talked about logging and mining. "Rainforests are being destroyed without considering the future."

Severn was the last to speak. "We'd like to show you some photos of my trip to the Amazon that inspired me to do something for the environment." She also included slides on the Sarawak jungle and ended by mentioning ECO's efforts to raise money for a water filter there. The applause was loud and encouraging.

"Well done, girls," the principal said as the room cleared. "You certainly have a flair for public speaking."

Michelle remembered Morgan's joke and laughed again. Soon they were all in stitches, all except Tove. As they walked to their class, Severn said, "See, Tove, you did just fine giving your speech."

"But I was so nervous, Sev."

"I was scared, too. It's weird presenting to people we know—especially our friends. My mom says it gets easier with practice."

"Maybe it will get easier for you, but I doubt it will for me. You've been on television. I'd never be able to do that in a million years of practice." Tove's voice was all chokey. "If we have to make more speeches, maybe I should quit ECO."

"But there are many other ways to help. My mom says that every person has special gifts to contribute. You are an artist and a hard worker and you love Nature. Those are all valuable qualities to have, especially in a group like ECO."

Good intentions are like pebbles tossed in a pool. Word of ECO spread like ripples. Each time the girls made presentations, they sold books, geckos, and baking. By the time the Penan men returned, ECO had raised several hundred dollars—enough to buy a water filter.

At a farewell event, the two men, Mutang Tu'o and Mutang Urud, were delighted to meet the girls who showed such care and compassion for their people. As they stood on the stage to present the money, Severn thought about her father's saying— You are what you do, not what you say. It felt so good to actually do something that would make such an important difference in the lives of Penan children halfway around the world. Imagine! Their contribution might even save lives.

In Borneo, Mutang Tu'o uses a long wooden pipe with a spearhead at one end to blow poisoned-tipped darts at prey.

CHAPTER 12
Hopeless

"There is a power in doing something that you believe in. We must find our real, basic values because once we are working within those values, nothing can stop us."

Severn Cullis-Suzuki

The steady slap of wipers in the spring rain had lulled Severn into a daze. Sarika drowsed beside her in the back seat.

"David, have you heard from Paiakan, lately?" Tara asked.

Severn's thoughts drifted back to the same drive they had taken to Quadra Island with Oe and Tania two years before.

"No, but I wonder if he's attending the Earth Summit in Brazil next year. They're expecting it to be the largest meeting of world leaders ever, much bigger than the first one twenty years ago."

"What's the Earth Summit?" Severn sat up straight.

"It's a gathering of heads of state and negotiators from each country; they're trying to figure out a way to deal with our environmental problems," her father explained. "It's a useless joke, really—a hopeless cause."

"Oh, David, we must have hope. Our leaders have to address these issues and try to find answers."

"Are you two going?" Severn asked.

"Not likely. I'm wary of these huge conferences. People talk, talk, talk. Then nothing changes." Her father shook his head. "Like I say, you are what you do—"

"—not what you say." Severn finished his sentence. "Are any kids going to this conference?"

"I'm not sure," her mother said. "Why?"

"Because I think all those grown-ups who are meeting and making decisions are not going to care about kids. If ECO went, we'd remind the leaders to think about our future for a change."

"I think you are absolutely right," her mother said. "I just don't understand why politicians are so near-sighted and don't consider that. Most are parents, too. I'm sure they love their children."

"Then why don't they start acting like they love us?"

"Action speaks louder than words." Her father repeated that phrase often, too. "I admire your desire to help the Earth, but believe me, going to the Earth Summit is a crazy idea. It will be a huge circus with thousands of people in a hot and polluted city. Besides, it would cost a fortune."

Sarika piped in, "Yeah, Sev. We can't save the Earth. It's hopeless."

Severn's parents glanced at each other and remained silent for a long time. Severn felt something heavy in the car, like the gray clouds hanging over the road ahead.

Then her mother spoke quietly. "It breaks my heart that you feel hopeless, Sarika. Daddy and I will try to be more careful about what we say in front of you. And it's not fair that you are so worried about the future, Severn."

"Not fair at all...." Her father's voice softened, too. "Your mother and I never had to think about these things when we were your age."

"You only have one childhood. And you'll be an adult far too soon. We want you to enjoy your young years," Tara said.

"We're very proud of the work you're doing with ECO, sweetheart." Her father smiled over his shoulder. "But try not to worry so much. Leave it to adults to be responsible for all these problems."

Severn slumped into the back of her seat and complained silently. *Leave it to the adults? But it's adults who are the problem! Don't they understand that the mess they leave behind will be our home one day?* Severn followed trails of raindrops on the glass with her finger. *Maybe it wasn't hopeless. Maybe there was a way to raise money to go to Rio.* She decided to tuck this idea away until the next ECO meeting. Her friends would think it was possible to go to the Earth Summit. For sure they would.

"Sev, that is positively the dumbest idea I've ever heard," Morgan said. "No way. Uh-uh. Impossible!"

Impossible. Severn didn't like that word. "Of course it's possible. We raised hundreds of dollars for the water filter."

"But we'd need thousands to buy plane tickets to Rio," said Vanessa, raising her eyebrows.

Michelle sighed. "Do you have any idea how many geckos that is? We could never make that many."

"But we're making them faster," Tove said. They now had a new assembly-line method of putting the pieces together.

Vanessa added, "And the Earth Summit is more than a whole year away."

"Be positive." Severn gestured with both hands. "We have to think we can!"

"Well, I think you're crazy, Sev," Morgan snickered. "But you know I like crazy."

"Well I'm also stubborn when I want something," Severn said, "and maybe I'm stubborn enough to make this crazy idea come true!"

David, Sarika, Severn, and the girls' grandfather enjoyed hiking in British Columbia.

BEATRICE LAKE TRAIL

CHAPTER 13

A Conscience to Adults

"We can't let the bad news get the better of us, and make us feel like our efforts are useless. We have to use the feeling of injustice and harness it to motivate us in speaking for our future."

Severn Cullis-Suzuki

"I'll race you back to the cabin, Sari," Severn said, swinging her pail of blackberries through the bushes. The sisters were enjoying the last delicious days of their summer vacation before starting third and seventh grades.

"I won!" Severn yelled, running into the kitchen. She plopped her pail in the sink then noticed their houseguest sitting alone at the breakfast table absorbed in a book.

"Sorry, Mr. Tompkins. I didn't mean to disturb you."

"No worries. Those look delicious."

Severn rinsed a few berries and put them in a bowl. As she brought them over to Mr. Tompkins, an idea flashed through her mind. Severn knew this man was very wealthy—not just because he had arrived in his own float plane, but also because he was interested in helping her parents set up a foundation.

"Mmm...thank you. There's nothing sweeter than a wild berry just kissed by the sun."

Severn took a breath before she plunged. "I think it's really great that you support environmental organizations. My friends and I have formed our own club, too."

"Is that right? Tell me about it." Mr. Tompkins listened intently as Severn explained ECO's interest in saving rainforests.

"You know, one of my ventures is buying large areas of wilderness to prevent the land from being logged."

"Just like the Children's Eternal Rainforest!" Severn tried to steady her voice and arrange her features to look mature. "Our big dream is to go to an international meeting where leaders will be making decisions about the future of the planet. We want to be a conscience to adults."

"Now, that's the kind of initiative I'm looking to invest in." Mr. Tompkins handed over his business card. "Write to me and tell me more about your plan."

"Thanks." Severn felt grown up just holding the card. She wondered if she should tell her parents. They still didn't know about ECO's plans to try to get to Rio. What if they disapproved? An inside voice said, *no, don't mention it*. At least not quite yet.

At the next ECO meeting, held in Vanessa's bedroom, Severn talked about writing Mr. Tompkins. "We need to explain why we think it's important for kids to be at the Earth Summit. I'll make notes."

"Dear Mr. Tompkins," Morgan said in a stick-em-up gangster voice. "Give us your money, or else!"

"This is serious," said Vanessa, stifling a giggle. If they cracked up, they'd never get the letter written. "First of all, we want to remind adults what's at stake if they don't change their ways."

"Yes," Michelle agreed. "Tell him we're worried about losing our future!"

"Right," Tove said. "Add that we think losing our future is way worse than losing money or elections. Adults should care more about us."

"But why should they?" Morgan snarled. "The future isn't theirs—it's ours."

Severn put down her pencil. "Let's tell him that kids want a future with whales and polar bears and rainforests for our own children to see. We don't want them to read about these extinct treasures in history books."

"And we don't want our air and water polluted, either,"

snapped Tove. "Let him know we're angry that they're wrecking the planet. We want the leaders to know how we feel."

"Slow down!" Severn yelped. "I'm writing as fast as I can."

"Also, say that we plan to do more fundraising, but his contribution will really help a lot," said Vanessa. "And add lots of pleases and thank yous. And draw peace signs, hearts, and smiley faces."

"I've been thinking..." Tove doodled with a pencil in her notebook. "Even if Mr. Tompkins gives us something, we'll still need to make more to go to Rio—a lot more. What we've collected so far is just a drop in the bucket. Are you sure we can do this, Sev?"

"Of course, we can do it. If Mr. Tompkins believes in us, others will, too."

"Hey, why don't we ask Jeff Gibbs for advice?" suggested Morgan. "He's offered to help."

"Oh, Jeff—Help! Help!" Michelle warbled in a high damsel-in-distress voice. "We know why you want to call Jeff."

Morgan hollered and slugged her with a pillow.

"Great idea. Let's ask him at

Severn's drawing of a howler monkey.

our next meeting at EYA headquarters," said Severn. "Hey, stop the pillow fight. We have work to do."

That night, Severn tried to sleep, but worries kept circulating like planets around the sun—big, small, near, and far. One minute, she was disturbed about the environmental problems they were writing about. The next, she wondered how five kids could raise thousands of dollars. Then she became anxious that Mr. Tompkins might be off on one of his world adventures. Or what if he sends a check and she has to give it back?

Another thought kept rolling around her brain—Tove's comment about the money they raised. "It's just a drop in the bucket." Her dad said that all the time when an action didn't make a bit of difference. Then she remembered a summer on Quadra Island when water had to be conserved because of a drought. Their kitchen tap was leaky so Severn put a pail underneath to catch the drops. A little while later, she checked the pail and it was almost full.

All those drops really added up fast. Maybe their drops in a bucket could make a difference after all.

The seventh-grade class of Lord Tennyson Elementary school.

CHAPTER 14

The Emperor Has No Clothes

"I think one of the most valuable lessons I learned
was how important parents are. Without their support
I couldn't have gotten as far as I did."

Severn Cullis-Suzuki

At ECO's monthly meeting at EYA headquarters a few weeks later, Doug brought in a stack of newsletters. "Your first issue hot off the press," he said, handing each girl a copy.

"Wow," Michelle exclaimed, flipping through the pages. "Good job, you guys."

"Now I'm a pro reporter!" Morgan pointed to her name in print.

"I'll take a bunch to our principal," said Vanessa. "He's offered to distribute them to other elementary schools, too."

When they finished admiring their work, Severn told Jeff and Doug about their dream to go to the Earth Summit.

Severn and the Day She Silenced the World

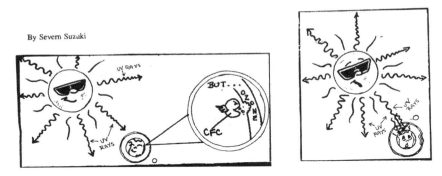

Severn's cartoon explained ozone depletion.

Tove created Envirowoman for the newsletter.

"Awesome idea," Jeff said. "We're hoping to send a rep as well."

"Got any bright ideas how we could make a pile of moolah?" Morgan asked. "I'm getting bored out of my skull making geckos."

"And look at my fingertips," Severn whimpered. "The skin's peeling off."

"We know a credit union that might help with finances," said Doug, picking up the phone. "Let me make an appointment."

"To raise money for the Penan we decided to plan one big benefit where lots of people could contribute," Jeff said. "It brought in a lot of dough."

"Do you think kids could organize something like that?" asked Michelle, wide-eyed with doubt.

"Why not?" Vanessa said, eagerly. "We could figure out how to do it."

"I'm sure our parents would help," said Tove.

Severn was about to agree, but before the words left her lips she remembered that her parents still didn't know anything about their plans. She wanted to tell them, but the time never seemed right. Then another worry zoomed into her head—they still hadn't heard from Mr. Tompkins. Severn felt a sudden jolt—an arrow of doubt had pierced her armor. The prospect of her dream coming true was not looking good. She knew that if ECO was going to go to Rio, she needed her parents' help. "I've got to get home for supper," Severn blurted, forcing a smile. On the walk home, she practiced the lines she would say to her mom and dad.

At dinner, Severn talked about the credit union. "Doug offered to help us fill out the application for a bank account to keep our donations...."

"Speaking of Doug," her father interrupted, raising an eyebrow. "This letter is addressed to you."

"It came!" Severn squealed, and tore open the envelope.

"Mom, Dad, look." She waved a check in front of their eyes, smiling smugly.

"A thousand dollars!" Her father's jaw dropped. "Holy cow—from Doug Tompkins? What on Earth...."

"Mr. Tompkins didn't think it was a crazy idea for ECO to go to the Earth Summit." Severn read from the letter. "Children should stand up and speak out for something important like their future." Then she bit her lip and searched her parents' faces for signs.

"I forgot all about your idea to go to Rio," her mother said, after Severn told them about ECO's letter.

"So did I." Her father put both hands on his daughter's shoulders and faced her squarely.

Severn looked him in the eye, straightened her back, and readied herself.

"I have to say, Sev, I'm astonished your gang took initiative and wrote a letter on your own."

Severn blinked. Was her father smiling?

"I'm really impressed." His head nodded up and down. "And proud!"

Severn recognized that look in her parents' eyes—they were seriously considering her plan.

"Maybe Sev is on to something, David. If children were to speak to leaders about the long-term implications of their decisions, people might listen—like the little boy who told the emperor he wasn't wearing clothes."

Severn's heart quickened at the turn of this conversation.

"Well I guess we could be persuaded to go to Rio as your chaperones..."

"Yahoo!" Severn shrieked before her dad finished. "You're going to help us?"

"Do we have a choice?" groaned her father with a crooked smile.

The next day, her mother suggested a family meeting to get down to the business of planning their trip. "I've made some quick calculations about the cost." Tara was always the one who planned their trips. "We could save money on hotels by renting an apartment for two weeks. Even so, the trip will be expensive—over fifteen thousand dollars. Do you have any idea how much that is? It won't be easy."

"I understand," said Severn, seriously, but the corners of her mouth spread into a wide grin. Now that her mother was helping, she could stretch out and almost touch her dream. Her mom could do anything!

"We also tried to figure out logistically how many people could go with us. We'll take Sari, so it isn't possible to invite all the girls in ECO," David said. "There will be tens of thousands of people at this conference and Rio is not a very safe city. You'll need strict supervision at all times. If you raise enough money to take one or two girls, we'll need another adult chaperone."

Severn's heart sank. When she played the dream in her mind, all the girls in ECO would attend. They were a team. They spoke together and wrote their speeches together, too. But Severn was too excited to think about that now.

"And while I still think you're crazy," her dad added, "we've decided to contribute one dollar for every dollar your group raises."

Severn grabbed Sarika and squeezed her tightly. That was some serious support for a crazy idea!

E.C.O. Helps the Penan

A Penan child

By Severn Cullis-Suzuki

The Penan are natives who live in Borneo, in the Sarawak rainforest with orangutangs, sloths, and many other animals. Today, along with monkeys and frogs, birds and lizards, the Penan are in danger of disappearing. Rivers are being poisoned by logging, because trees cling to soil and when those trees are cut down, the soil, sometimes containing poisonous minerals, washes into the water. Children and animals get sick from drinking the polluted water. A lot of animals exist only in the Sarawak rainforest and nowhere else. Now, if too many animals die from drinking this water, they will become extinct, forever.

E.C.O. helped the children in the rainforest stop getting sick. Not completely, because rivers are being polluted in many places in the forest of Sarawak, but E.C.O. bought a water filter to clean drinking water for one of the many Penan villages.

Unfortunately, animals and the Penan are still getting sick. E.C.O. helped by getting a water filter, but still the rainforests of Borneo need a lot of support to be saved.

ADDRESSES TO WRITE TO IN MALAYSIA:

1. Prime Minister of Malaysia
]Prime Minister's Department
Jalan Dato Onn
50502 Kuala Lumpur
Malaysia

2. Cheif Minister of Sarawak and Minister of Resource Planning
YAB Tan Sri Datuk Patinggi
Abd. Taib Mahamud
Cheif Minister's Office
Bangunan Tunka Abd.
Rahman Putra
Petra Jaya, 93503 Kuching
Sarawak, Malaysia

Severn wrote about the Penan in the ECO newsletter.

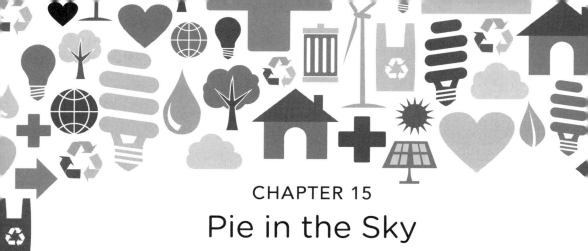

CHAPTER 15
Pie in the Sky

"Something kids can do to take action is write letters to people, politicians, and companies who are treating the planet badly."

Tove Fenger

"This is absolutely, positively the most incredible possibility in my whole life," Morgan swooned, collapsing in her chair at their meeting table. Since hearing that David and Tara were attending the Earth Summit and matching ECO's donations, Morgan's mood was not nearly as grumpy.

"I'm sorry we can't all go," Severn said, wistfully. "But the important thing is to have an ECO representative who will deliver our message to the leaders."

Vanessa was bubbling with excitement, too. "If only one or two of us can go with you Sev, how will we decide?"

"Well Tove was the original member," said Morgan. "And she's made more geckos than anybody."

"But you're a better speaker, Morgan," Tove said. "I get so nervous in front of crowds. And I've never traveled to South America like Michelle."

"How much have we raised so far?" Michelle asked.

"About three thousand dollars," Morgan said, then wagged her finger. "Sev, if you think we can raise thousands more you are nutty as a fruitcake, certifiably insane, crazy as a loon, cuckoo, fruit loopy—"

"But with David and Tara match-ing it, that makes six thousand," Vanessa said, brightly.

"Whacko, bonkers, delusional," Morgan continued. "Off your rocker, 'round the bend, a raving lunatic!"

Michelle said, "Remember what Jeff said about organizing a big event?"

Tara walked in carrying a tray with five slices of pie. "Jeff's right. A large benefit is a terrific idea."

Morgan's eyes lit up. "Mmmm... pie," she said, drooling.

Tove Fenger was the shyest ECO member.

David popped his head around the corner. "Tell me if you girls think that my pumpkin pie isn't the best you've ever tasted."

"A fundraiser is something I could help you with, if you like," Tara offered.

Severn admired that whenever her mother met a challenge, instead of becoming overwhelmed, she decided what she could do and then figured out how to do it. "If plan A doesn't work, there are twenty-five more letters in the alphabet," she would say whenever Severn felt discouraged.

"We have to fill out this conference application." Severn squished her eyebrows together as she glowered at the papers.

"I can help explain it to you," said Tara. "According to my research, there are actually three conferences. Rio Centro is

Severn takes a break from writing for the ECO newsletter.

where the government leaders are meeting. Non-governmental organizations, or NGOs like ECO, are at the Global Forum at another location. The Earth Parliament is for those not invited to the other two."

"But we want to be

near the leaders," Severn said, firmly. "They're the ones who need to hear our message."

"Well, you have to be invited to speak at Rio Centro. Don't worry. You'll meet important people at the Global Forum and the Earth Parliament."

At the next meeting, Tara proposed a plan. "The Vancouver Planetarium rents its auditorium. There's a screen for showing slides—an ideal place for a large function."

"Sounds perfect, Tara," Vanessa said. "We'll ask our parents to invite everyone they know."

"I can make posters," said Tove. "I'm sure EYA will offer to photocopy them."

"Your friends and family can help poster them around town," Tara continued. "It's important to get started on publicity right away."

"And make more geckos," Michelle sighed.

"We can also sell coffee and cake," Tara added. "I'll print up some blank checks to make it easy for people to donate."

"Clever!" said Morgan. "No one can use the excuse, 'Sorry I left my checkbook at home.'"

Vanessa asked, "So how do we get people to write us checks?"

"Think about exactly why you want to send an ECO representative to Brazil. Write it down," Tara said. "You need to be convincing."

"And we need to give a dynamite presentation," said Severn. "The best one ever."

"Well, you know that speaking isn't my thing," said Tove, meekly, "so I'll support you with other stuff, like drawing pictures and creating the slide show."

Severn's stomach folded. "But Tove, giving speeches is the whole point of going to the Summit."

Tove slouched in the chair, her hair draping her face as if she was trying to disappear. In a little voice she said, "Then maybe... maybe I shouldn't go with you."

Severn tried to protest but a giant lump stuck in her throat. It was difficult to see Tove struggling with the decision. Although she couldn't imagine being in Rio without Tove, Severn was beginning to think that maybe it was for the best if Tove decided not to go. But how could she do the most important thing in her life without her best friend by her side?

Trying to change the world was proving to be complicated.

RIGHT: Michelle encouraged kids to put solutions into action to improve the environment around them.

WHAT YOU CAN DO...

By Michelle Quigg

Now that we know the problems, we need to find solutions. There are many simple ways that you can help the planet. A helpful hint may be to work with some of your friend's (ideas come more easily). Once you have formed your group, you can then start on thins to do.

You've probably heard of the 3 R's Reduce, Reuse and Recycle. By doing the 3 R's you can cut down on the household garbage because garbage dumps are beginning to take too much space.

Certain things that may normally be thrown away can be recycled like, paper, tin cans, glass and cardboard. If you separate these materials, they can be taken to a recycling depot and be reused once again instead of being wasted.

For things you can't recycle try to reuse in things like art creations. You can compost food scraps to create healthy soil for your garden.

Also if you see things around you that may harm the environment like the pollution in rivers and lakes, make your city mayor aware of the situation by writing a letter explaining how it may effect other life forms, like fish and tell them you would like something done about it.

There are many environmental problems, pick one you find important and then think of all the creative solutions to solve it. Finally, put your solutions in action to improve the environment around you.

Published by E.C.O. in association with the EYA:
P.O. Box 34097, Station D Vancouver, BC V6J 4M1 Canada
SUPERKIDS: Severn Cullis-Suzuki, Tove Fender, Morgan Geisler, Michelle Quigg, Vanessa Suttie
SLIGHTLY MORE AGED HELPERS: Susan Kurbis, Erin Wallace
THANK YOU TO OUR FUNDER: VANCITY SAVINGS CREDIT UNION

PLEASE GET IN TOUCH!

You can write to us at

Environmental Children's Organization
c/o the Environmental Youth Alliance
P.O. Box 34097, Station D
Vancouver, BC
V6N 2G1

Send us your ideas, articles and questions. We would love to hear from you!

ECO Newsletter Subscription Form

☐ Yes, I would like to continue receiving the ECO Newsletter. Enclosed is a cheque for $10.00, for the next 3 issues. (Please make cheque payable to the Environmental Youth Alliance.)

☐ Here is my donation of $_____

Thank You for your interest and support

Name: _____
Address: _____
City: _____ Postal: _____
Phone #: (___) ___ - _____
School/Group: _____

Published as an Environmental Youth Alliance Educational Report. Vol. 2, No. 6, March 1992

Printed in Canada
Printed in Vancouver, B.C.
Environmental Youth Alliance
PO Box 10497
2405 Pine St. Station D
V6J 4M1
Second Class Registration no. 8725

Environmental Children's Organization

FUNDED BY

VanCity

Right now we have to change and stop making mistakes, but the question is: "How?" Anger and helplessness can't solve anything. The Environmental Children's Organization is a kids group that isn't just standing around anymore watching as people destroy our World.

E.C.O. does what it can to help the environment, even helping people half-way around the World. We have also been trying to get the message across that children will have to live in the mess that some adults are now making.

In the last two years, seven kids have raised enough money to buy a water filter for the Penan Natives of Borneo. The Penan's water is getting more and more polluted by logging. To buy this filter E.C.O. sold jewellery that we made ourselves. Also, we have been talking at high-school meetings about the problems in our World; what we have done to help and giving slide shows. We have proven to ourselves that, when we work together, it is possible for children to help our World.

We know there are a lot more kids like us out there. The next step is to join together. The more of us that work together, the more we can accomplish. It is up to us. It is our planet and our future.

Severn Morgan Vanessa
Michelle
Tac

CHAPTER 16

Help us Change the World

"I always thought that when I grow up I want to have an impact in the world. I want to make a difference. I want to do something. But I've already begun to make a difference—I think mainly because I haven't grown up."

Severn Cullis-Suzuki

"Whew! I had no idea a benefit would be this much work," Morgan said to Vanessa and Tove as they biked to the planetarium. The girls had been busy leading up to the big night—putting up posters, inviting people, printing pamphlets and programs, recruiting volunteers to bake goodies, and of course, making more ECO geckos.

"So much for a relaxing March Break," Vanessa sighed. "At least we were able to practice our speeches."

"Holy, cow! It's packed," Severn gasped, as she handed out programs to people streaming to their seats. She noticed that the audience was mostly adults, not the students and teachers she

THE EARTH'S FATE;

A CHILD'S VIEWPOINT

The Environmental Children's Organization (ECO) invites you to a children's view on our planet's future,

March 17, 1992 from 7:00 to 10:00pm at the auditorium in the Planetarium.

The earth is in peril, but it's the children who will have to live with results of decisions, whether bad or good made by leaders of our world. Please support us.

Features:

an ECO slideshow from our view of the world

and a speech by David Suzuki, Andrea Miller (W.H.E.N.) and other guests.

Price is $5 for seniors and students and $8 for adults. Your contributions will help ECO go to Earth Summit, a conference of worldwide leaders discussing the Earth's fate in Rio de Janeiro. It is all of our future, and children especially have the right to have a say.

tickets available at door or
by calling
263-8110 or
EYA Number: 737-2258

was used to. Severn fidgeted with her bracelets until the lights dimmed. Then Vanessa began to speak.

"Hello everyone. Welcome to the event we have called, The Earth's Fate, a Child's Viewpoint. I will be your emcee for the evening—and that's not my rapper name—I'm Vanessa Suttie."

As people chuckled, the other girls entered the stage. Severn began, "Imagine that you are in the Amazon, the largest remaining rainforest in the world. You are surrounded by the sounds of the jungle, cicadas humming, birds chattering. You are far away from the city, but the forest is loud. Suddenly, the rain begins to fall."

The girls walked around, rubbing their palms together, encouraging the audience to do the same. "The rain mist dampens all the plants of the forest." The girls snapped their fingers. "Now the rain is falling harder." Larger droplet sounds rippled around the room. Next, they patted their legs and drummed on their thighs making the sound of pounding tropical rain.

Then the girls stomped their feet, like a real Amazonian downpour. The entire auditorium became the deep wilderness of South America. Then, they went back through the actions, the ripples of changing rain, and finally the rain receding into mist once again. The girls were astounded—their piece worked better than they had ever imagined. The evening was ready to begin.

Severn felt unnerved knowing people were watching, but their faces were in the dark. As soon as she began to talk about the Amazon, her tension vanished.

"A few years ago, I had the incredible opportunity to visit the Kayapo people of the Brazilian Amazon." Tove showed slides—the beautiful forest, the Rio Zinho, the Kayapo—ending with the plumes of smoke.

"This is why I care about decisions made about our environment. The burning forest is like an enormous palace covered in flames. Not only the kingdom burns, but all the valuable things inside. In the end, the palace is gone. It is the same with the rainforest; millions of innocent animals are left extinct or without a home.... If action against the destruction is not taken, you will only see these animals in the pages of a storybook."

When it was Vanessa's turn to speak, her papers quivered but her voice was loud and clear. "My talk is called, My Hopes for What We Can Do About It." She told the audience about the United Nations Conference on Environment and Development (UNCED), the proper name for the Earth Summit, and why ECO wanted to speak to world leaders there.

At intermission, the girls raced to their table in the lobby where people were lining up to buy items.

"We need change," Tove said, in a panic, holding up a twenty dollar bill.

"Keep the change." The customer flapped his hand. "It's for a worthy cause."

"Hey, baby beluga," said a man with twinkling eyes and a black beard.

"Raffi!" squealed Severn, giving her friend a hug.

Morgan's eyes bulged. Raffi was a megastar. All Canadian kids knew his songs "Baby Beluga" and "Wheels on the Bus." Usually a chatterbox, Morgan could not utter a single word.

Raffi smiled and picked out a few pins. "I'm proud of you girls. This work is so important."

Michelle grabbed Severn's arm. "You never told us you know Raffi!"

"He lives around the corner from us. Raffi's involved in the environmental movement and he's a supporter of my dad's new foundation." As Severn turned and ran toward the auditorium, she shouted, "Never mind star gazing—you're giving the next speech."

Michelle talked about how shocked she was to witness the terrible living conditions in Colombia, a country plagued by civil war and drugs. "Poverty causes poor countries to destroy rainforests. Leaders should help people and the environment instead of spending money on wars."

The speeches closed with Morgan. "I'm going to talk about the problems I see in my own backyard and how what's happening in British Columbia will affect our future." At the end, she said, "You'll notice that we placed a blank check on your seat—hint, hint! If you didn't notice, it's probably all sweaty and squished so we have fresh ones at our table." When the laughter subsided, Morgan asked for donations to buy airfare to Rio. "We ask you," she said, pointing into the audience, "to help us change the world."

Raffi models a Kayapo headdress—much to Severn's amusement.

At the end of the presentations, a man jumped onto the stage. "I'm holding five two-hundred-dollar checks that I will donate if others match them." Severn's grandfather was the first to hand the man a check.

A woman shouted, "I'll give another." Before long, two thousand dollars was raised—just like that! Severn marveled at how her mom's suggestions had paid off. People were very generous.

When everything was cleaned up and packed, the girls sprawled on the floor, exhausted.

"Are you too tired to count your donations?" asked Michelle's mother, Patricia. The girls bolted upright and watched as Morgan counted out bills and Patricia tallied the checks with a calculator. "Four thousand, seven hundred dollars!"

"Whoa Mama!" exclaimed Morgan.

"Raffi gave me this before he left." Tara waved a check for four thousand dollars. "And he said you'll see him in Rio."

"Yay, Raffi!" Vanessa exclaimed, jumping up and tapping a victory dance. The others joined in until they fell down laughing.

"I have the grand total," Patricia announced. "With the proceeds from tonight, plus the private donations, and all the money the girls have raised so far, the total is...."

The girls stopped their giggling and started to bounce. "What? What is it?"

"Oh, Mom, tell us!" Michelle cried.

"You've raised more than... thirteen thousand dollars."

Severn was stunned.

All eyes turned to David.

"Oh boy, I know what you're thinking," he said, running his fingers through his unruly curls. "I said I would match your earnings." He took an exaggerated gulp. "I guess this means ECO's going to Rio!"

Rio de Janeiro, Brazil

The friends held hands and twirled, chanting, "We're going to Rio!"

"Me, too," shouted Sarika. "Me, too!"

"Of course, Little-Me-Too." Morgan brought Sarika into their circle. "You're officially an honorary member of ECO."

Without warning, Severn's heart plummeted. The application! She hadn't received the confirmation yet. What if they were turned down? Severn thought about warning the girls not to get too excited, but they were so happy. All she could do was paste on a smile. And wait.

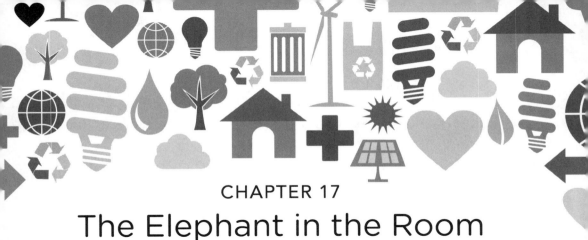

CHAPTER 17

The Elephant in the Room

"In your heart, in your child's heart, you know what values, what principles are right."

Severn Cullis-Suzuki

"The girls will be here soon for our planning meeting." Tara was making a pot of herbal tea. "The decision needs to be made about who will be going with us."

Severn had been so thrilled with their success, she had pushed that thought to the very back corner of her mind. "How many can go?"

"Well, we never expected that you would get so many donations. Now it's possible to take three girls."

"But what if we raise more money so we can all go?" As Severn pleaded, she knew this was impossible. The Earth Summit opened in just over two months.

"Sev, if everyone came we'd have to take another chaperone and rent another apartment. There's nothing available at this late date."

Severn jumped at the ring of the doorbell. Tove, Vanessa, Morgan, and Michelle kicked off their shoes and headed straight to the dining room table. The cups rattled on the tray as Severn carried in the tea and cookies. "Our handouts have arrived." Her voice sounded a little too cheerful. As the girls looked them over, her mother pulled up a chair.

"I have terrific news," Tara said. "Michelle's mother has agreed to be a chaperone to supervise when David and I are attending meetings and giving speeches. Patricia speaks Spanish and understands some Portuguese, which will be a great asset."

"Fantastic," said Morgan. When her Mom was working, Michelle's place was her home away from home.

Tara described in more detail what to expect in attending a large international conference and the challenges of traveling in South America. "This will not be a fun vacation. You'll work harder than you've ever done before. Your job will be to talk to strangers all day. With luck, you'll give live radio and television interviews, and make speeches to large crowds. It will be stifling hot and crowded with tens of thousands of people. And we are worried riots might break out with protestors. Tensions are running very high even before the Summit has begun. You must be absolutely certain that you can handle this commitment."

"Thanks, Mom. We'll talk about it." Severn turned to her friends. "I wish we could all go."

"But we knew that we'd have to decide," Michelle said. "At least now, three of us can go with you instead of one or two."

Morgan was the first to speak her mind. "Well, I'm not afraid to give speeches. And I want to go to Rio more than anything else in the world!"

"I'd love to go, too," Vanessa said, "but, we all want to. Maybe we should draw straws."

A heavy silence filled the room like an elephant. Finally Tove spoke. "I'm not sure a straw vote is the best way to decide. Tara's right—we need to choose the best speakers." She stared into her hands cupped on her lap. "I'm just not sure you can depend on me."

Then Morgan blurted, "I know that you've made more geckos than anyone and you've really worked hard to raise money, but if you're not absolutely sure about speaking, Tove, then maybe you shouldn't go."

Severn opened her mouth to protest, then stopped. Was it fair to disagree with Morgan for saying out loud the very same thing she was thinking? Michelle and Vanessa didn't say anything, either. Did that mean they were agreeing with Morgan?

"The most important thing is to get our message out to the

leaders—that's why we've worked so hard all these months," Tove said, avoiding all the eyes holding her. "It's obvious that you are all better speakers. I should be the one to stay home."

Severn's heart tugged. Her friend was so strong. She couldn't imagine making the same sacrifice.

Michelle and Vanessa's shoulders drooped. Morgan stared down. Not a word was uttered.

The awkward silence was interrupted by David who appeared with a large brown envelope. "This letter is addressed to ECO."

"It's from the Summit!" Severn exclaimed, tearing open the envelope and scanning the page. "It's official. We've been assigned our very own booth."

Severn closed her eyes and felt the weight of all the worries on her shoulders lessen. She was sad that Tove wasn't able to go with them, but at least the decision had been settled. And ECO was now registered as one of the thousand delegates. In two months, they would be in Rio, telling the leaders of the world to pay attention to children.

E.C.O.

he Road to: RIO

WHEN ECO FIRST PLANNED TO GO TO RIO DE JANEIRO TO ATTEND THE EARTH SUMMIT, MY FIRST IMPREESIONS WERE: "NO WAY, UN-UHN!" (I DIDDN'T THINK WE WERE GOING TO MAKE IT). BUT AFTER OUR FUNDRAISERS AND THE UN-STOPPABLE WORK OF DAVID AND TARA SUZUKI (SEVERN'S PARENTS), WE MADE IT DOWN. OUR GOAL WAS TO REACH POLITICIANS AND REMIND THEM THAT THEY ARE MAKING DESISIONS FOR US, THE CHILDREN, NOT THEM, SINCE WE ARE THE FUTURE AND THEY'LL PROBABLY BE DEAD ANYWAY.

TO GET THAT MESSAGE DOWN TO RIO WE NEEDED TO FUNDRAISE. WE HAD A SLIDESHOW AT THE PLANETARIUM TO RAISE FUNDS AND AWARENESS FOR OUR CAUSE. WE HAD BAKESALES, BOOKSALLES AND DONATIONS FROM VARIOUS GROUPS, INCLUDING THE DAVID SUZUKI FOUNDATION. AND ALL THIS TO GET DOWN TO RIO, TO THE

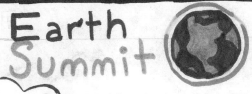

Earth Summit

WE MADE IT !!

WE SURE DID. THIS SCRAPBOOK IS TO SHOW OUR ACTIONS AT THE EARTH SUMMIT, THE EARTH PARLIMENT AND OUR BOOTH AT THE GLOBAL FORUM. (BOOTH #66, SECTOR YELLOW, TO BE EXACT!) I TRIED TO RECALL AND WRITE DOWN ALL I COULD, BUT IO HOPE MY MEMORIES WILL FILL IN WHAT MY JOURNAL ENTRIES COULD NOT. SO... ON WITH THE SHOW!

Morgan Geisler kept a diary of her ECO trip.

E.C.O. Going to Brazil

By Severn Cullis-Suzuki

In story books you can find pictures of beautiful Brazilian rainforests. The Amazon is inhabited by millions of different animals, birds, insects, monkeys and many more. Despite their presence in the story, these amazing animals were not born in the pages of a book. Their real homes are far, far away in the Brazilian rainforest. Unfortunately, in Brazil there are many poor people. Children there don't worry about getting to school on time or brushing their teeth, they worry about having a place to sleep and finding food. Money is desperately needed to fight this poverty, and the Brazilian government has been logging the forest to earn money by selling the giant trees.

The burning forest is like an enormous palace covered in flames, not only the kingdom burns, but all the valuable things inside. In the end, the palace is gone; it is the same with the Brazilian rainforest, and millions of innocent animals are left extinct or without a home. Eventually they disappear, and if action against the destruction is not taken, you will only see these animals drawn in the pages of a story book.

Instead of watching the forest being destroyed, many people will gather in Brazil to attend a meeting called the Earth Summit. E.C.O. is going to be there too. The purpose of this meeting is to think of ways to help our sick Earth, to put bandages on the holes in the ozone layer, and to restore the disappearing forests. E.C.O.'s message at the conference will be different than most groups. We are children who will have to live on the Earth no matter how dirty or beautiful it is. This is our Earth too, and we should be able to help decide what will happen to it.

All people want a healthy planet, by working together, adults and children alike, we can ensure that children everywhere have a future to look forward to.

Severn wrote an article for ECO's newsletter about the trip to Brazil.

CHAPTER 18

On the Road

"Maybe the most important thing children can do is influence their parents, because moms and dads love us more than anything."

Severn Cullis-Suzuki

"There it is—Rio de Janeiro!" Severn exclaimed, pointing to the distant cluster of skyscrapers, nestled between jutting mountains and the Atlantic Ocean. As the city came into view, all the frenzy of the last months vanished. ECO's crazy dream had come true.

"It's like a sea of many colors," Morgan said, marveling at the lush hues of land and water below.

"It's kind of like Vancouver," Vanessa proclaimed, "only more beautiful."

That beauty soon faded as the plane flew over an expanse of

The favelas of Rio de Janeiro climb the city's hills.

drab, boxy shacks, that looked as if a huge dirty quilt had been dropped on part of the city.

"It looks like a town that's been flattened by an earthquake," Morgan said.

"Those are the *favelas*," Severn said, "where the poor people live."

"People actually live there?" Vanessa gasped.

The wheels on the landing gear thumped the tarmac. When the plane came to a stop, the ECO girls cheered the loudest of all.

"Stay together, girls," warned Patricia, as they streamed toward the baggage carousel.

Morgan laughed nervously. "I feel like a salmon swimming upstream."

The crowds were worse than at the other Brazilian airport. Severn wondered if all these people were attending the Summit.

"Whoa, Mama!" roared Morgan, as they hit a wall of sizzling air outside the airport terminal.

"It's even hotter than Colombia," Michelle moaned, wiping her forehead. Her mother flagged two cabs. The travelers piled in, four to each cab, squeezing their luggage into the trunks.

As they rode the highway lined with palm trees and flowering bushes, they came to the favelas. The girls had a closer view of the ramshackle houses cobbled together with wood and terracotta bricks, topped with corrugated tin and clay tiles. They were stacked haphazardly one on top of another climbing up the steep hills, looking as if a strong wind might topple the homes like a stack of cards.

David became more and more anxious as the cab swerved in and out of traffic, brakes screeching, horns blowing, ignoring all the highway lanes. He snapped at the driver for speeding, wiping sweat from his brow. "I told you this would be a nightmare!"

Severn clung to her dad, heart in her throat, certain they were going to crash. She didn't admit that Rio was scary—she was starting to understand why he didn't like crowded cities.

"No wonder the air is so bad." Morgan faked a choking fit. "I've never seen so many cars."

Elegant mansions and high-rise office towers soon replaced the slums. White stucco apartment buildings crowded the endless gleaming white beaches dotted with umbrellas and sunbathers. Finally they reached the apartment that would be their home for the next two weeks. Once they hauled their bags up to their suite and beds were claimed, the girls admired the view from the balcony.

"It's a very famous beach," Tara said, "the Copacabana."

"Let's go swimming," cried Sarika, jumping like a Mexican bean.

"Sorry, sweetheart. This beach is not safe for swimming. The water's polluted with sewage," said her father. The girls groaned. "And the police have warned us about muggings."

"Muggers and turds," Morgan muttered. "Mom will be so happy when I tell her!"

"Besides, we need to find your booth," said Tara.

"But I'm starving!" Severn whined. The other girls pulled hungry faces, too.

"We'll pick up some food on the way," David said.

The stores were closed for mid-day siesta, but there were many street stands that sold clothing, food, and all sorts of other items. Morgan held up a bikini. "This is not a bathing suit—it's dental floss." The girls fell into fits of laughter.

"Food! Glorious food!" Morgan sang as they passed stands that sold rice and beans, octopus, squid and spiky crabs, potatoes and chicken. The smells made their stomachs grumble even more. "Hard-boiled quail eggs? I'm feeling adventurous."

As the girls stood in line for food, a crowd of ragged children surrounded them holding out grubby palms, pleading for change.

"Why aren't they in school?" asked Vanessa.

"They're street kids," said Severn, wishing she had some change. The kids looked hungry.

"I've seen street children in Colombia, too," said Michelle. "They have really challenging lives. Some scavenge through dumps just to survive. Sometimes they're forced to be child soldiers or sell drugs."

Sucos bars had every exotic fruit drink imaginable; flavors the girls had never tasted before.

After they finished their lunch, the group took taxis to the Global Forum. As the cabs snaked past rows of tents and through hundreds of people, Tara struggled with maps and diagrams to find ECO's booth.

"This is a circus," David complained through clenched teeth. The humidity had made his hair even more wild and curly.

"Oh, Pops," Severn said, rolling her eyes. "Try to chill."

"Don't I wish. Rio is like a raging inferno!"

"There it is," shouted Tara. "Number 66. The Environmental Children's Organization."

"It's real," breathed Severn. A tingly current surged from her head to her toes as she stood before their space. Her thoughts scampered over all the steps they had taken to reach this spot.

"I don't think we'll all fit at the same time," Michelle looked at the small table and three folding chairs, then at all their stuff.

"Not unless we pack ourselves in like sardines," Morgan said. The tent was barely nine feet (three meters) wide.

"It's good that we're on a corner." Vanessa was chipper as usual. "We can talk to people inside and outside the tent."

"Make sure you wear hats and sunscreen at all times," said Tara as the two women flopped in the chairs, fanning themselves with ECO newsletters.

"Yes, my fine freckled-friends." Morgan pointed to her sun hat.

"Hey, look who's talking!" Michelle snapped.

"This isn't the time for a freckle contest," said Vanessa. "We have work to do."

"We'll hang posters and photos on the wall," said Severn, emptying a box, "and put our newsletters and handouts on the table." As she lifted the two banners her mom's friend had sewn, Severn was reminded of how kind and supportive so many

Sarika, Severn, Morgan, and Michelle
needed a break after setting up their booth.

people had been. Then she took out some colorful signs and posters. "Tove made these for our booth."

"They're beautiful," Morgan said, holding a handful of geckos. Then her smile collapsed. "I never should have told Tove she shouldn't go." Her voice trembled as if she was going to cry. "It's all my fault she's not here—because I'm selfish!"

In an instant, Severn was also fighting back tears. She wanted to tell Morgan that it wasn't her fault, but she kept busy instead, pushing upsetting emotions away. "Let's put the green and blue banner at the top so that everyone can see it," she said, forcing a cheerful tone. Vanessa brought chairs for them to stand on. Michelle unpacked the staple gun and duct tape. Severn was relieved that no one mentioned Tove again.

It took some time to set up the booth, but everyone was pleased when they finished. "Ours looks just as nice as the others," said Severn, proudly.

"Even better," Morgan cried, her voice sounding brave. "Now, on with the show!"

CHAPTER 19
Attracting Attention

"I wonder sometimes if adults in their complicated and busy lives forget the simple things."

Severn Cullis-Suzuki

"Wake up, girls," called Tara. The sun streaming through the blinds already promised a sweltering day. "We need to get cracking. It's your first day to tell the world about ECO."

Severn's body felt glued to the mattress. "Ow!" she cried as Sarika climbed over her on bony knees.

Morgan was already up and dressed, gaping at a bowl piled high with pineapples, mangoes, and papayas. "Wow! I'd have to rob a bank to buy this in Vancouver."

The girls were still yawning in the cabs as they headed to the Global Forum. Today the site was even busier. People were speaking a million different languages and wearing unfamiliar clothing and adornments—hats, head coverings, hairstyles—from all around the globe.

"I don't see any Kayapo," Severn said.

"They're at the Earth Parliament several miles from here," her father said. "It's just nuts that the world's First Nations are excluded at these conferences. The decision-makers could learn from the people who have a better understanding of—and a lot more respect for—Earth."

"So they might not get to meet world leaders, either," Severn muttered under her breath. Then she remembered to be positive. We *will* meet leaders, she told herself.

"We'll visit the Earth Parliament on Children's Day next week," said Tara, before she and David left for meetings.

Morgan folded her arms and looked at the booth. "We'll have to take turns being on duty."

"We should write a schedule," Severn suggested.

"Good idea!" Michelle picked up a pen and paper. "When we're not working we can explore."

"You must stick together," Patricia cautioned. "Keep your map with you and don't wander far away."

"*Bonjour, Madame.*" Severn handed a flyer to a woman in an orange sundress, their first official visitor. "*Je m'appelle Severn.*" She talked about ECO and why they had come from Canada. The woman smiled. "*Merci, et bonne chance.*"

"It helps that we all speak French," said Vanessa. It was also useful that Severn remembered a little Portuguese and Michelle spoke Spanish.

"I think being young helps, too," Morgan said. "It attracts attention, then we can—*pow!*—sock our message to 'em."

The Global Forum had just started and already the girls were getting visitors who were interested in knowing what kids were doing at this serious conference. All day long, they talked to people, posed for photos, and gave interviews to reporters from around the world, even a crew from their home media, the Canadian Broadcasting Corporation (CBC).

"I'm impressed." A reporter flipped through the ECO material while the photographer took pictures. "Did you girls write this?"

"We did," said Vanessa. "We have something to say."

"We also raised the money to come here," said Severn, proudly, "with help from our community."

"And what made you decide to come to the Earth Summit?"

Michelle said, "We want to talk to the leaders who are here to make decisions."

"People don't think of children as important for these meetings, but the choices that adults make today will affect the rest of our lives," Severn added.

"Decisions made here will affect the future, and we are the

future generation." Morgan leaned on the table with crossed arms. "We are going to be tomorrow's adults and that's why we have such a big stake in this. We want to remind these old geezers to think of us, the children, not just themselves." Morgan flipped her hand. "And they'll probably be dead, anyway."

The reporter laughed. "And how do you like Rio so far?"

"Well, it's very, very hot and crowded," Vanessa said. "And it's weird seeing police with guns and clubs on every corner."

"And the favelas were shocking," Michelle added, "to see

Vanessa and Michelle speak with reporters about ECO.

so much poverty and then to see the rich homes with guard dogs to protect them."

"We're doing a longer story on the street people near Rio Centro," the reporter said. "They were rounded up and dropped off in the slums so they wouldn't embarrass the government in front of thirty thousand visitors."

The group is ready for action at ECO's booth. From left, Patricia, Morgan, Vanessa, David, Sarika, Severn, Michelle, and Tara.

"That's so not fair." Morgan flipped her hand. "Sweeping their dirty secrets out of sight."

"It's just occurred to me, we could also do a story about ECO at the Earth Summit. Would you like to come with us on a tour of the favelas? After, you could tell us your impressions."

"That would be very interesting." Severn sounded calm, but inside her heart was skipping double-dutch. "We'd love to."

"And we're also covering a huge protest march in a couple of days. We could interview you about that."

The girls grinned and linked arms. Severn said, "Our ECO adventure just keeps getting more exciting!"

On the ride home, Michelle said, "Whew, that was a lot of work." It was hot and humid, and they had sore feet and hoarse throats. And, as always, the gang was hungry and thirsty. They were looking forward to sampling some local specialties at a restaurant that night. At the Brazilian *churrascarias*, waiters came to the table with towers of barbequed meats on skewers—even hearts and livers and all kinds of cuts the girls had never seen before. The waiters shaved off slices of meat with long swords.

Morgan's eyes and mouth popped open. "Too bad for the vegetarians."

"I say, too bad for the animals," Vanessa said, sarcastically.

"And the planet," Severn added. "Remember that clearing rainforests for cattle isn't very environmentally friendly."

"Yeah," Morgan snickered. "Especially with gazillions of cows farting methane gas."

"Morgan! We're eating here," Michelle wailed.

Vanessa rubbed her hands together when the side dishes arrived—cube fries, onion rings, peas and beans, a strange looking corn, and salads. The waiters asked, "Si?" or "Nao?," but the answer was always "si." It didn't take long before everyone was stuffed. There were lots of leftovers to take with them.

As they walked back to the apartment, a few gaunt children trailed behind. Michelle put her fingers to her lips and handed them the leftovers.

Morgan, Vanessa, Severn, and Michelle enjoy Brazilian cuisine.

When they arrived, Sarika pleaded, "Can we play on the beach, now?" The others joined in. "Please? Please?"

"After all your complaining I thought you'd want to go straight to bed." Tara placed her hands on her hips. "Well, I guess you've earned some beach fun, but no going in the water."

David looked anxious, as usual. "Stay close to us at all times."

"Don't worry, Pops," Severn said. "If we stray, just yell onça-pintada."

Beach fun was the perfect way to end the day and burn off steam. The girls did cartwheels, ran races, twirled until they were dizzy, and buried themselves in the sand.

CHAPTER 20
Puzzle Pieces

"A lot of things you can do seem so insignificant but when everyone does them, it really adds up."

Severn Cullis-Suzuki

"*Shame! Shame! We're burning up!*" Raffi's voice sang out loud over the din of the parade. He had arrived in Rio the night before and joined the girls and parents marching down a wide seaside boulevard toward Rio Centro. *"Earth is dying. We need action."* Severn, Morgan, Michelle, and Vanessa clutched the raspberry banner and chanted the protest slogan Raffi had written for the Earth Summit. *"Shame! Shame! We're burning up."*

Thousands of environmentalists streamed along singing, clapping, beating drums, carrying signs, and shouting slogans to send messages of concern to the world leaders. Never before had Severn experienced such a huge and thrilling event. She was like a small piece of a gigantic puzzle—and every piece was just as important as all the others.

The CBC crew interviewed the girls as they marched. "It's great to see all these people out here—we all have the same ideas about protecting the environment," Vanessa shouted over the noise.

Michelle said, "It's really exciting participating in such a large a global event."

Severn gripped their banner, aware of how easily she could be swept away by the tsunami wave of protestors. The heavy police presence made her edgy, too, as if at any time the protest could turn ugly. She imagined how freaked out Tove would have been in the midst of this pulsating noise and throngs of people. For the first time, Severn was relieved she wasn't with them.

Thousands of protestors marched down the Avenida Atlantica in Rio.

When the march was over and they were leaving to get to their booth, the girls said good-bye to Raffi. "Bye-bye baby

132

belugas. See you later at the Earth Parliament. I hear you're giving speeches."

"Are you singing one of your new songs?" Morgan asked, looking hopeful. Raffi's latest album was an environmental collection called *Evergreen Everblue.*

"I didn't bring my guitar. Hey, maybe we can sing 'Shame! Shame!' after your speech."

Vanessa pulled a face. "I don't mind making speeches, but singing?"

"It won't be so scary if we're singing together." Severn slung her arm around Vanessa's shoulders.

Later, after they had arrived at the booth, Tara hurried over, flushed. "The Canadian Minister of the Environment is coming."

Finally! Severn's heart swelled as she saw the Minister approach—their first chance to speak to someone really important.

"Bonjour Monsieur Charest." Each girl shook the Minister's hand, pleased to speak his first language.

"What grade are you in?" he asked.

"Grade seven."

"I guess you are happy to be missing school. Are you having fun? I bet. Where do you live? Ah, yes, I love Vancouver. What are your favorite subjects in school? Make sure that you do your homework while you're here."

The girls answered each question politely, waiting for a question about ECO.

A man with a clipboard tapped the Minister on his sleeve. "Well, it's always wonderful to see fellow Canadians at these global events. *Au revoir!*"

"What...?" Severn's mouth dropped as Monsieur Charest strode away. "We didn't get a chance to discuss anything important."

Severn and Vanessa speak with Canadian
Environment Minister Jean Charest.

Vanessa complained, "He just wanted to talk, not listen to our ideas."

"We weren't taken seriously at all." Michelle crossed her arms. "He treated us like cute little girls."

So is this is what politicians are like? Severn wondered. She wasn't impressed.

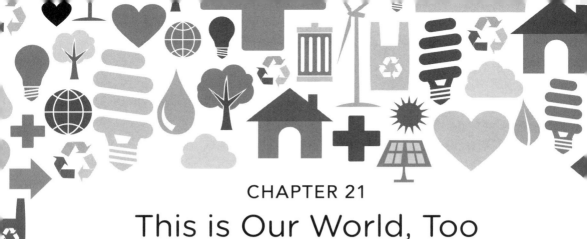

CHAPTER 21

This is Our World, Too

"I came here today because I have nothing to lose except my future. I ask politicians not to throw my future out the window."

Vanessa Suttie

As each day went by, the girls attracted more and more attention. They handed out stacks of leaflets and exchanged addresses with other youth keen to set up their own ECO clubs. At the end of a long day, Morgan said, "People are saying 'I love that you're taking action' and 'I love that you're not leaving it all up to the adults.'"

Severn said, "It really bugs me when they say, 'We've really messed up the world, but now we can relax because children like you are our hope. You're going to save the world.' I feel like yelling, 'So does that excuse you from acting? How can we be different when you are our role models?'"

"Most people believe in the same things we do," Michelle said. "It's the politicians we need to talk to."

"At least people are listening to us," Vanessa said. "They're telling others to come to our booth and we're getting more media attention."

"Yeah, but a lot of the reporters still ask dumb questions about school and homework and how young we are—just like the Minister did," complained Morgan. "But I'm getting better at steering them to what I want to talk about—the important stuff."

"Politicians do that all the time," Severn said. "I think we're improving our public speaking with all this practice." That was true. They were receiving invitations to speak at side events at the Global Forum. Usually only one or two girls could speak for a few minutes, so they began taking turns.

Severn and Morgan work on homework while Sarika takes a nap.

David arranged some opportunities, too. "I'm giving a speech at the Canadian Consulate. I think ECO is the most interesting thing at this conference. Would you like to speak during my slot?"

"Would we ever," the girls said together.

"Finally!" Severn exclaimed. "A chance to speak to the people with power."

Morgan put her hands on her hips, and growled, "Will the Canadian Environment Minister be there?"

"He sure will. I bet he won't brush you off this time," David said. "You'll need to shorten your speeches and cram all the things you want to say into a few minutes. Can I help?"

"Sure." Morgan handed David a newsletter. "You can be my fan!"

The next evening, David took the girls to the consulate. On their way to their seats to listen to the speeches, they passed a refreshment table filled with Styrofoam plates and cups, and plastic bottles of water.

"And they call this an environmental conference?" Morgan muttered. The girls shook their heads and rolled their eyes.

One of the speakers had been at the UN environmental

conference that began the movement in 1972. He talked about how promises had been made, but not kept. Severn thought about her dad's common complaint: talk, talk, talk, and no action. This time was going to be different.

After a brief speech, David said, "Now you should hear from the ones with the most at stake in all that's going on here." The girls filed to the podium.

Vanessa spoke first. Only her friends could tell she was nervous.

"I came here today because I have nothing to lose except my future. I ask politicians not to throw my future out the window," she began. She ended her speech with this reminder, "The decisions made here will affect children around the world."

Next up was Michelle.

"In Canada we live the privileged life...yet in Colombia I see children my age on the streets...begging for money, living in shacks, with no sewers or water. I can't stop thinking that I could be one of those children...I am here in Brazil to tell the leaders of the rich countries that we don't want to be so greedy anymore."

Morgan expressed similar concerns.

"Canadian children aren't aware of the inequity between the rich and poor....We just naturally assume that everything is a fairyland—that all children have a place to sleep, food to eat, and adequate clothing.... We believe that Canadian children have a responsibility to share what they have."

When it was Severn's turn, she made sure that she spoke firmly and clearly to get her message across.

"Right now you have to stop making mistakes and make change for the sake of our future. We have to live in the mess that you are making. We're not going to stand around and watch you destroy our world."

The audience cheered. Cameras flashed. Reporters rushed to the stage for interviews.

Then Minister Charest shook their hands warmly. "*Merci* for your efforts."

"I'm glad to have this opportunity to talk to you personally," Morgan charged in boldly. "I didn't get a chance to say this before, but when you're making decisions about the environment, remember who you're making them for. This is our world, too."

"*Monsieur, do you have children?*" Michelle took courage from her friend.

"*Mais, oui.* Three young girls." The Minister smiled. "It is important that you get a chance to speak and we get a chance to hear. We are all thinking about our children. When you speak, we not only hear your voice, we hear the weight of your words."

When the Minister left, Morgan high-fived each girl. "Now that's more like it!"

The first week at the Earth Summit flew by. Tara was right. The girls worked harder than they had in their whole lives. At the end of every day they were exhausted, but there was always something to do—writing speeches or in their journals, laundry, showers, and of course, homework. And the gang headed to the beach whenever they had the chance.

But it was frustrating not being able to swim in the ocean, so one day before going to their booth they traveled up the coast to visit some university student delegates from Canada for a morning by the water. When they arrived at the pristine beach, Severn and Michelle charged right into the waves.

"Did you check the water for any turds?" Morgan was stalling.

Vanessa plunged in backwards. "Come on, Morgan, it's fun!" A huge wave lifted and launched her forward. "I thought you were the brave one!"

Morgan finally mustered her courage and dove in. When a group of oily, tanned young women wearing string bikinis

Severn clowns around
with Michelle and Vanessa.

Vanessa and Severn finally get to swim in the ocean at San Conrado.

passed by, Morgan called out, "Does anyone need any dental-floss? Those ladies brought some."

The girls laughed uncontrollably, hoping none of the bathing beauties spoke English.

In the bus on the way back, the girls soaked up the enthusiasm of the university students who were heading to a press conference where they'd hear the official youth delegation's speeches later that day.

"I didn't know that young people were officially part of the Summit," said Severn. "That's awesome."

"Three hundred people who are age thirty and under from ninety-seven countries spent a week in Costa Rica preparing a Youth Statement for Rio," said one of the students. "Their delegation was designed to replicate the real world: the percentage of indigenous participants reflected that of the global population, as did the ratio of rich to poor—and there were equal numbers of males and females. They dealt with important issues, from poverty to pollution."

"They get to speak for only an hour—one hour out of fourteen days—big deal!" muttered one girl. "And youth under thirty represent half of the world's population."

"It's better than nothing," Tara said.

When they arrived at the Global Forum, David said, "Morgan will be speaking at another press conference this afternoon. Maybe we'll see you later."

"How did it go?" Severn asked, when her father and Morgan came back to the booth.

"I was almost arrested, that's how it went!" Morgan bellowed, flopping into a chair like a drama queen.

David explained. "We arrived at Rio Centro just after a riot broke out. Apparently, the youth who had been scheduled to speak were told they only had ten minutes, so tensions were pretty high. Then two minutes into their Youth Statement, the TV cameras were turned off. When the speakers tried to tell the press, the UN police dragged some of them away and arrested them."

"Why did they cut them off?" asked Tara.

"For being too radical, I guess. They suggested canceling

Third World debt because rich countries exploited the poor countries enough during the time of colonialism."

"There was broken glass and kids were on the ground crying—some were beaten by the police." Morgan was breathless. "And then the guards wouldn't let us in because they thought we were part of the protest. Luckily, my hero David was eventually able to convince them we weren't involved. I arrived just in time to give my speech."

Severn remembered her mother's warnings of danger at the Summit. But she had never really expected violence like this—especially against young people who were only speaking up for what they believed. Severn could only imagine all the work it took to write their statement—only to be denied their freedom of speech. How disappointing!

Now it was even more important for ECO to address the leaders at this conference.

CHAPTER 22
Shame! Shame!

"Fighting for the environment is very exciting. By working on various projects I've met wonderful people and from my experience I look at the world in a different way."

Severn Cullis-Suzuki

"Woo-hoo!" Morgan tickled her friends out of deep sleeps. "It's Children's Day."

"Leave me alone." Severn pulled a pillow over her head.

"It's too early," Michelle groaned. "Get lost, Morgan!"

"I asked Morgan to wake you all up," Tara said. "We have a full day ahead."

"I've arranged an opportunity for ECO to speak tomorrow." David poured a coffee. "It's at an event hosted by Maurice Strong."

Severn knew he was the Secretary General of the UN

conference and a fellow Canadian. She grinned, thinking about all the important leaders they'd meet.

"It's a press conference about education and ethics."

"A press conference?" Severn's shoulders dropped. "But that's just for reporters."

"Yes, but there are over ten thousand reporters in Rio. This is a golden opportunity to get your message out to the public." David took a sip of coffee. "It's a panel so there will be time for only two of you to speak. Whose turn is it?"

"I spoke yesterday," Morgan said. "Remember—when I was almost thrown in jail!"

Vanessa said, "Severn and Michelle are up."

But first there was the Earth Parliament. On the way there, Severn asked her parents, "Will Paiakan be here today?"

Her mother bit her lip. "Paiakan planned to come, but we read newspaper headlines saying that he was arrested."

"It's probably just trumped-up charges to prevent him from speaking," her father said, bitterly. "The Brazilian government doesn't like activists, especially indigenous activists."

"Oe and Tania must be so scared." Severn tried to imagine her own parents being thrown in jail, or worse. She knew that another Brazilian environmental activist, Chico Mendes, had been murdered a few years earlier. A sob escaped from her throat.

"Oh, sweetheart, we didn't mean to upset you." Her father stroked the long braid down her back. "I'm sorry we told you about Paiakan."

Severn flopped her head on his shoulder, trying to hold back tears. "I just don't understand why there are so many problems. They all seem so scary and big."

"Yes, it's true," her mother sighed. "Such things can be overwhelming, for sure. I wish we could protect you from knowing about the troubles of real life." Her voice brightened. "But think of all the inspiring people we've met here who are doing incredible things to make the world a better place."

Tara's positive outlook usually cheered Severn and encouraged her to face challenges. But today she couldn't brush away her gloom. It wasn't just worry about Paiakan. She was also thinking about leaving Rio in a couple of days. They hadn't met any world leaders yet. Severn wanted to talk to her own Prime Minister and the President of the United States. Soon it would be too late.

When they arrived at the Earth Parliament, Severn was shaken out of her doldrums by pulsating drumbeats and joyful singing. Here was some soul for the Earth—and color. People wore all kinds of clothing and adornments—feathers and paint on different Amazonian tribes, bright colorful African caftans, American Native regalia, and everything from suits to jeans.

David, Raffi, and the ECO girls were ushered onto a large stage. Before their speeches, the emcee gave the girls instructions. "Make sure you pause after each sentence to give the translator time to repeat your words in Portuguese."

Raffi pointed to a man in the audience dressed in a T-shirt and jeans. "He's an important American senator—Al Gore. He's written a book called *Earth in the Balance*."

Severn stood taller. This brought ECO one step closer to the President of the United States!

After an amazing show of indigenous grass dancers below the stage, David spoke. "I'd like you to hear from someone who will be inheriting the problems facing Earth, problems we have created—my daughter, Severn Cullis-Suzuki."

Severn stepped toward the mike while her dad adjusted its height. She exhaled a deep breath she didn't know she was holding. *Don't blow this*, she urged herself.

"Hello, I'm speaking for ECO—The Environmental Children's Organization. We are a group of twelve and thirteen-year-olds from Canada trying to make a difference."

Severn paused for the translation, keeping her expression serious.

"I'm just a child and I don't have all the solutions, but I want you to realize that you adults don't either. You don't know how to fix the holes in the ozone, or bring salmon up a dead stream, or bring back animals now extinct. I am asking you—if you can't fix it, don't break it!"

Vanessa was next. She talked about how worried she was about the future.

"Losing my future is not like losing points on the stock exchange or in an election. We as children are not easily heard. Our opinions are just as important as [those of] our Canadian Prime Minister Brian Mulroney or the U.S. President George Bush."

Morgan spoke about why ECO thought it was important to be in Rio. "Do not forget why you're attending these conferences, who you're doing this for—the children."

Michelle spoke last. She ended with:

"I'm here in Brazil to tell all the leaders of the rich countries that we don't want to be so greedy anymore, to forgive the international debt, and to share our technology freely."

The audience clapped enthusiastically. It was the perfect time to launch into their song. Raffi turned to face the girls and hummed a note. Then he started clapping to the beat.

Shame! Shame! We're burning up.

Earth is dying. We need action.

Shame! Shame! We're burning up.

Severn couldn't believe it. They were actually performing with Raffi. This was awesome!

Reporters interviewed Severn after her speech at the Earth Parliament.

When they finished, the CBC and other reporters rushed to the girls for interviews. Minister Charest came over to introduce several delegates. "This is Mr. James Grant, the head of UNICEF in the United States."

Severn struggled to keep from bouncing with joy. "I'm pleased to meet you."

"I was very moved by your speech, Severn." Mr. Grant clasped her hand. "Is it possible to get a copy of it? I am meeting with your Prime Minister, Brian Mulroney. I'd like to give it to him."

Severn's heart turned a cartwheel. "Of course." She tried to smooth her crumpled paper before handing it over. "Sorry it's messy."

"Are you sure you want to give me your original copy?"

"Sure, I won't be needing it. We're leaving in a couple of days." As the words left Severn's lips, the end of the conference suddenly became even more real. Maybe this was the big break she had been waiting for. ECO's message was reaching at least two very important world leaders. Their mission was accomplished!

Morgan met a Kayapo delegate at the Earth Parliament.

But the show wasn't over. The girls returned just in time to watch a group of young people dressed in ragged costumes perform a dance. Severn's eyes pooled with tears. The children's movements described their difficult life—delivering a more powerful message than all the speeches they had heard that day. At the end, one of the dancers took off his clothes.

"I wasn't expecting that," Morgan whispered, surprised but not shocked.

"I wonder if they're showing us that the children are made to feel that they don't even have a right to clothes," said Michelle.

Severn was curious to learn more about these struggling children. Tomorrow they would have that chance.

CHAPTER 23
Dreams and Hopes

"We believe that Canadian children have a responsibility to share what they have."

Morgan Geisler

"The CBC van is here." Tara shooed everyone out of the apartment, down the stairs, and into the van. The reporter introduced the social worker who would be their translator and guide. They drove past the clean, modern city center, into a slum area behind some brick and glass office buildings and shops. The van maneuvered through narrow garbage-strewn laneways spray-painted with graffiti, past a cardboard box with pairs of tiny bare feet protruding from the end. They stopped at a park where the group left the van.

"*Hola*," the social worker said to some kids who were passing around a cigarette butt. She asked if they wouldn't mind being interviewed. As the reporter dropped coins into their outstretched palms, Severn thought they seemed stunned and spaced out. She suspected they might be high on drugs.

"The kids are upset and scared because someone has just threatened to kill them," said the social worker.

Vanessa was shocked. "Can't the police give them protection?"

"No they can't. In Rio, sometimes it's the policemen who murder children," the social worker explained.

The reporter asked a boy called Fabio, "Why are you living on the street?"

Fabio's vacant gaze turned bitter. "My stepmother chased me with a hot iron. She threw it at me so I ran away. Now I get chased by the police, but I can run fast."

A boy dressed only in shorts stiff with dirt said, "The police rounded us up like dogs and moved us here."

"They beat us with clubs." A smaller boy showed bruises on his back and legs. "They threatened to shoot us but we jumped out of a window. Now my family is very hungry while all those rich people eat big fancy meals."

"Our parents don't have money to feed my brothers and sisters." A girl named Racquel kicked the spindly grass. "Before, I asked tourists for money. But in this slum there are no tourists."

Severn noticed that some kids weren't much taller than

Sarika. "We're twelve and thirteen," she said in Portuguese. "How old are you?"

The tallest boy said, "Seventeen." Fabio was fifteen. Racquel was twelve.

"That's crazy!" Vanessa whispered. "I thought I was short for my age."

"Malnutrition affects their growth," the social worker explained.

"Where do you sleep?" Severn asked.

One boy motioned for them to follow. He led them down a grubby alley to a shed. The social worker translated for them, "It's an abandoned construction trailer. Thirty kids sleep there."

Stinking garbage swarming with flies was piled outside the door. *Please don't gag*, Severn told herself. Inside, were more piles of garbage. Then she realized that this must be all of their belongings. Severn tried to keep a pleasant expression on her face to hide her horror. It was their home, after all.

Michelle had turned the color of chalk. "I feel faint, Mom," she mumbled, and then left abruptly.

"We should leave, too," Tara said, taking Sarika's hand.

"Not yet," Severn said. "This is important."

Vanessa motioned to a hole in the floor. "That's their toilet," she whispered, holding her hand over her nose. The social worker turned and led everyone outside.

Morgan summoned courage to ask, "What are your dreams and hopes?"

Smiles lit the children's faces. "We wish to be rich."

"And if you were rich, what would you buy?" asked the reporter.

"I'd give all the street children food and clothes and medicine," said Racquel. "We'd all have a nice house and live with our families and they would love us and give us affection. No one would beat us." The other children nodded.

The Brazilian children posed with the girls after their meeting.

Severn, Morgan, Michelle, and Vanessa's eyes met, silently sharing their sadness. Then the street kids waved good-bye and ran off to spend their coins.

As the girls all expressed how awful they felt about the living conditions of the kids, the social worker explained, "Yes, it's very frightening. Some adults even poured gasoline on them while they slept and set them on fire. Some were burned badly." She shook her head. "There are millions of children and teenagers living miserable lives in conditions with no water, no electricity. Sometimes they are violent because violence has been their only experience in life."

The reporter asked the girls, "What is your most vivid impression of what you just experienced?"

The street children slept in a shed with all their belongings.

"It's terrible. I can't believe this is actually happening." Vanessa held a hand to her chest. "I know I'm so fortunate to live in Canada, but lots of people don't realize how lucky we are to have a house to come home to and food to eat."

"Some children's homes are no more than wood and paper boxes," Severn said. "These children have nowhere to go, nowhere they are wanted. They really made us think."

Morgan's words tumbled out. "I take music lessons for granted. I take school for granted. I take everything for granted. When I meet kids who can't go to school, I realize how many privileges I have. These children are just as important as any other person in the world."

"We come down here and say, 'you've got to save this tree and this plant,'" Vanessa motioned with a clenched fist, "but we really have to save these children!"

"It's hard to imagine that they could be killed," Severn said, solemnly. "They could be dead in the morning. They have no control over their future and I think everyone in the world should have at least some control over what's going to happen tomorrow."

When they returned to the van, the girls talked about how ECO might be able to help the street kids once they returned to Vancouver.

"I know ECO is all about helping the environment, but I never realized how important it is to help people living in poverty, too," said Vanessa.

Morgan said, "If kids' lives are in danger and they have to scrounge for food in garbage dumps, I can understand that living in a polluted city is not their biggest worry."

"It's poor kids who suffer most from an unhealthy environment," Michelle said.

"If poor Brazilians were able to feed their families, they wouldn't need to burn down the rainforest." Severn shook her head. "You can't blame them for wanting to rise out of poverty."

"The wealthy nations want to impose environmental regulations on poor countries," Patricia added. "But the poor countries feel that would limit the rise of their standard of living."

"True," Tara said. "And that is the drama unfolding at the heart of the negotiations—the tensions between rich countries who have money and poor countries who want money."

Severn thought, there was that word again—*money*. If rich countries want environmental protection, they should pay for it, especially since they consume way more natural resources and cause more degradation. Wasn't that only fair?

But these issues were so complicated!

"Thank you, girls," the reporter said, when they dropped the gang off at their booth. "It's been wonderful getting to know you and following you around for the last few days. We wish you the best of luck and hope you get to speak to the UN."

The gang poses with the crew from the CBC.

CHAPTER 24

It Doesn't Seem Fair

"We have proven to ourselves that when we work together it is possible for children to help our Earth, even help people half-way around the world."

Michelle Quigg

The next evening, David sat at the end of a long table at the press conference hosted by Maurice Strong. "Michelle, sit beside me. When you've finished, Severn will take over. Good luck! You'll blow everyone away." The others sat in chairs with the reporters.

Michelle took the microphone. "My name is Michelle Quigg. I was born in Canada…I am also part Colombian and have been fortunate to visit Colombia several times. I would like to share my impressions of the contrast between North and South America.

"In Canada, we have a privileged life with plenty of food,

water, and shelter. We have watches, computers, television sets, and cars that make our life easier. Every day I wake up and go to school knowing that when I return home, I will have food on the table...In Colombia and Brazil, I see children my own age living on the streets...begging for money; nine-year-old boys carrying bricks and planks of wood too heavy for their young bodies to support; children filling potholes and shining shoes, living in houses of bags and roof shingles.

"While flying into Rio, I saw the favelas—countless shacks with no water or sewage treatment, which in Canada we take for granted. I can't help thinking...that it makes a tremendous

Michelle is speaking at the Education and Ethics panel.

difference where you are born. I could be one of those children in the favelas of Rio, a child starving in Africa, a victim of war in Somalia, or a beggar in Colombia. It doesn't matter where we live. Children are children with the same hopes and dreams.

"In Canada many people are overweight...Meanwhile, millions of innocent people suffer from malnutrition. People in Canada use stationary bikes to lose weight, then get in their cars and drive to work. It doesn't seem fair to waste while the world starves. In Canada we have many desirable accessories, but this comes at the expense of poorer countries. We hoard many of the Earth's resources to make us happy, but we also make the South suffer...I want to share my wealth...Why can't adults share as well? We never seem to be satisfied with what we have, we always want more for ourselves. But we must break this selfish habit...Any child can see that we need to share. Thank you."

Severn gave a speech similar to the one she had given at the Consulate.

"Parents have always been able to comfort their children by saying, 'Everything will be all right' or 'We're doing the best we can'. But you can't say that to us anymore. Our planet is becoming worse and worse for all the children, yet we only hear adults talking about disagreements and national priorities. We hear a lot of talk about the First World, the Second World, and the Third World. But all my life, from space satellite pictures I've only ever

Severn spoke last on the
Education and Ethics panel.

seen one world; and because we are only one Earth, whatever happens in India, China, or Brazil will affect all of us in Canada, Europe, and Japan."

People clapped and cameras flashed. David beamed widely. "Great job!" he said, squeezing their hands.

Morgan, Vanessa, and Sarika congratulated them, too. Severn was proud that she and Michelle had delivered their speeches so well. But something didn't feel quite right. Sure she was happy, but a part of her felt empty—as if something was missing. Was it Tove? Was she still disturbed about the street children? Were their words enough to make a difference?

David was happy too. "You have all worked like crazy and talked to a ton of people, way more than most participants." He hugged each of them. "Congratulations!"

"We are very, very proud of what you've accomplished," Tara added, "and you all should be, too."

Her mother was right—ECO had achieved so much. Severn thought about all their fundraising in Vancouver; running their

Severn says hi in their Global Forum booth.

booth for almost two weeks; speaking five minutes here and there at all the different venues, and the countless interviews in four different languages. So what if they hadn't been able to speak to the United Nations and the world leaders?

"Well you have certainly earned a few days in the Brazilian Rainforest as a reward," Tara said, reminding the girls they had to pack for their trip to the Ariau Jungle Towers.

"Woo-hoo!" Morgan hollered. "Amazon Rainforest—here we come."

Tara took the girls on a ferry ride on the weekend.

CHAPTER 25
Telling the World

"We have to stop, and think about what is really important to us."

Severn Cullis-Suzuki

"I'm so excited to see a real rainforest," said Vanessa, stuffing clothes into her suitcase.

"You'll be blown away." Severn zipped up her bag. "We'll even get to sleep in a wilderness tree house."

"We'll see monkeys and butterflies and parrots," Sarika said, "and alligators."

"Alligators!" cried Morgan, lifting Sarika and twirling her around.

"Alligator pie, alligator pie! If we don't get some we think we're gonna die!" The girls all chanted together.

"Shhh!" Tara put a finger to her lips. "The phone's ringing."

"Hello. David Suzuki speaking.... Yes. I see."

Severn caught a glimpse of her dad's expression. He seemed surprised, cheeks round and happy. He covered the phone and whispered loudly, "Kids, there is an opportunity for Severn to speak at the last plenary session at Rio Centro! There's a five-minute spot."

"Whoa Mama!" Morgan exclaimed.

"This is so awesome." Michelle slapped her cheeks.

"When?" Tara's voice was weighted with concerns.

"Early this evening."

"You mean when we are at the airport waiting for our plane?"

The girls jumped up. "Forget about the plane. This is why we came to Rio!"

David returned his attention to the phone conversation, then hung up.

"So what happened?" Severn was practically bouncing.

"Well, James Grant—remember the head of UNICEF?—bumped into Maurice Strong and suggested that you speak at a plenary session. Then today someone dropped out of the agenda."

"So he wants me to speak?" Severn clasped her hands to her chest. Then she let them drop. "But we always take turns. I gave a speech yesterday."

Michelle stepped forward. "But Sev, this is your dream. We

wouldn't be here without you."

"And you are the best speaker," said Vanessa. "We don't mind. Honest!"

Severn turned to Morgan. Behind her expression, it seemed as if hamsters were running inside wheels in her brain.

"Well, Sev, I am insanely jealous, but..." She broke into a silly grin. "Of course you should be the one."

"I'll see if we can change our flights and hotel bookings." Tara had already picked up the phone. "Then we'll call a taxi."

"This speech has to be the best one ever." Severn's stomach lurched. "Oh no! I gave my last copy to Mr. Grant. We don't have time to write another."

"Of course we do," said Michelle, calmly searching for her own speech. "If we do it together it won't take long."

"We know exactly what to say," Vanessa assured her. "We've been talking and making speeches for two whole weeks."

"You can do it." This time her father was the positive one.

Severn hugged herself and sighed. "You guys are truly the best."

"You have to keep it short—under four minutes," David warned. "That's not much time."

"I know, Pops."

"And make sure you mention the really important messages, like pollution and wildlife. And future generations—"

"Dad, I know what to say." Then Severn felt badly for cutting him off. "When we're finished, you can give me pointers how to say it out loud."

"Sorry, Sev. I only want to help."

"Great!" Morgan handed him a newsletter.

"I know, I know. I'll be the fan."

"Success! The arrangements have been changed." Tara hung up the phone after a marathon of calls. "Now, let's get down to the taxis. We don't have much time."

Vanessa, Michelle, and Morgan sat in the backseat of one cab. Severn and her dad squeezed in the front. She took out the new speech already cluttered with crossed-out sections and scribbles in the margins, arrows, and notes all over. As Severn read through it, the girls added their favorite points here and there. It was their final, ultimate ECO collaboration. But it was difficult to write in the car—Severn felt every bump and pothole in the road. Her paper was very messy.

"Are you sure you can read that?" her father yelped, glaring at the crazy papers.

As the taxi cab swerved and wove through traffic, the girls worked away at the speech, oblivious to the driving that had scared them out of their wits only two weeks before. "Are we late?" Severn asked frantically, pushing damp tendrils away from her eyes. The stifling heat and humidity made her hair frizzier than usual. "I won't have time to rehearse."

"You've got this one, Sev," Michelle said, with confidence. "No problem."

Finally, the taxi slowed down in front of a long, white building surrounded by menacing army tanks—the Rio Centro compound. Soldiers with intimidating glares stood guard around the entrance, machine guns held at the ready. Severn's heart

Sarika, Severn, Morgan, and Vanessa managed to talk
one of the armed guards into posing with them.

was really pounding now. She was relieved to see the other taxi had arrived. Her mother had already found the right entrance. A uniformed official studied their passes and read through a long list of names of people permitted to enter. Severn braced herself for the bad news—her name wouldn't be there. Then he nodded and directed the group toward the security check.

"Oh, bliss." Severn sighed as they entered the building. "Air-conditioning!" Even her papers were sweaty.

The group had to move quickly through the hallways. Magically, they found their way to the UN Plenary Session.

"It's huge," Morgan gasped as they walked into the conference room. There were seats for hundreds, but only a few dozen people sat in the rows of chairs, grouped by country. "Where are all the delegates?"

"I guess people are tired of sitting through two weeks of meetings," whispered Michelle.

Severn felt an extreme sense of calm flood over her. The last ten days had been like a practice for this very moment—this had been in her dreams and she knew what came next. It didn't matter that the room wasn't full. Every person here was an important decision maker.

Raffi joined them. "Are you okay, baby beluga?"

"I'm nervous," Severn said, "but I'm not scared."

"Just remember, keep your head up," Raffi tilted her chin a

little, "and look into people's eyes. It's important to make eye contact."

Severn was about to speak to the leaders of the world. She glanced around—at her ECO friends, her family, Patricia, and Raffi. All these wonderful people were lifting her up. As she walked to the stage, Severn felt them beneath her, carrying her forward.

One of the organizers seated Severn at the back of the stage with three girls from other environmental organizations—one from Germany, one from Guatemala, and one from Canada. *It's wonderful that the delegates are hearing from children today,* Severn thought. *But I hope we aren't just token characters to them.*

"Keep your speech to three or four minutes," the organizer said. Severn gulped. Her speech was longer. She stared helplessly at her scribbled notes. What could she leave out? What if they cut her off before she finished?

One by one, the girls walked to the

Severn felt nervous but calm as she took the stage.

front of the stage and spoke about their hopes for the future—for better care of resources, the protection of wildlife, the right to clean water, and the importance of education for children around the world. The girls were sincere and respectful, and made suggestions for solving the world's problems. The audience nodded and smiled. Their applause was polite.

Then Severn's name was called. She walked to the podium and found her family in the audience. Her poor dad—she could tell he was terrified. Her mother and Sarika were smiling, we love you. At that moment she felt a surge of strength and confidence.

Severn raised her chin and looked directly into the eyes of one delegate and then another. She took a deep breath.

"Hello, I'm Severn Suzuki speaking for ECO—The Environmental Children's Organization."

Severn saw her beautiful ECO friends who had dedicated so much time and effort to this crazy project.

"We are a group of twelve and thirteen-year-olds trying to make a difference: Vanessa Suttie, Morgan Geisler, Michelle Quigg, and me. We've raised all the money to come here ourselves, to come five thousand miles to tell you adults you must change your ways."

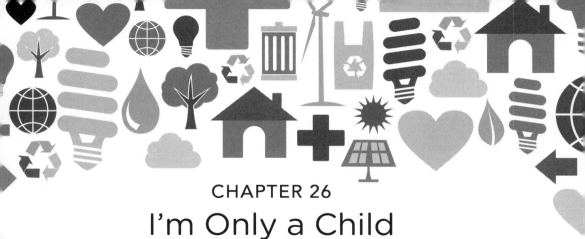

CHAPTER 26

I'm Only a Child

"On behalf of her generation and those yet to come, Severn's strong call for change is unique in its logic and in its moral voice. Her speech deserves to be read by everyone."

Raffi

One hundred and eight world leaders had gathered at the Earth Summit in Rio de Janeiro on June 3, 1992, to discuss ways to protect our beautiful planet from human destruction and figure out an action plan for a more responsible future. Scientists had warned that if environmental problems were ignored there would be dire consequences—rising oceans, changes in weather and climate, air unfit to breathe, polluted water and land, the thinning of our ozone layer, and the disappearance of vital species. Indigenous leaders had reminded industrialized countries of the importance of caring for Earth—the mother of us all—the one who nourishes and sustains us.

On June 12th, after hundreds of speeches, meetings, and side events, the delegates were saturated with tough information and disheartening statistics. They were tired and discouraged with the lack of progress in the negotiations at Rio Centro.

In the noisy corridors bustling with people, delegates mingled and shuffled from appointment to appointment, occasionally glancing at the monitors broadcasting the speeches from the plenary sessions. But something on the screen caught the attention of a few delegates and then a few more. A child. A child in a flowery top speaking into a microphone, her voice calm, passionate, innocent. People slowed their pace. Sentences of conversation were left dangling.

"Coming up here today, I have no hidden agenda. I am fighting for my future. Losing my future is not like losing an election or a few points on the stock market. I am here to speak for all generations to come. I am here to speak on behalf of the starving children around the world whose cries go unheard. I am here to speak for the countless animals dying across this planet because they have nowhere left to go.

"I am afraid to go out in the sun now because of the holes in our ozone. I am afraid to breathe the air because I don't know what chemicals are in it. I used to go fishing in Vancouver, my home, with my dad until just a few years ago we found the fish full of cancers. And now we hear of animals and plants going extinct every day—vanishing forever.

"In my life, I have dreamt of seeing the great herds of wild animals, jungles and rainforests full of birds and butterflies, but now I wonder if they will even exist for my children to see. Did you have to worry of these things when you were my age?"

Crowds assembled around the monitors to hear this girl who spoke with a child's voice—but clearly and powerfully. The halls fell silent. A woman, who had a daughter about the same age, dabbed her eyes with a tissue. Men cleared their throats.

"All of this is happening before our eyes and yet we act as if we have all the time we want and all the solutions. I'm only a child and I don't have all the solutions, but I want you to realize, neither do you!

"You don't know how to fix the holes in our ozone layer.

"You don't know how to bring the salmon back up a dead stream.

"You don't know how to bring back an animal now extinct.

"And you can't bring back the forests that once grew where there is now a desert.

"If you don't know how to fix it, please stop breaking it!

"Here, you may be delegates of your governments, business people, organizers, reporters, or politicians—but really, you are mothers and fathers, sisters and brothers, aunts and uncles— and all of you are someone's child.

"I'm only a child, yet I know we are all part of a family five billion strong, in fact thirty million species strong, and borders and governments will never change that. I'm only a child yet I know we are all in this together and should act as one single world toward one single goal. In my anger, I am not blind, and in my fear, I am not afraid of telling the world how I feel.

"In my country, we make so much waste. We buy and throw away, buy and throw away, buy and throw away, and yet northern countries will not share with the needy. Even when we have

Severn challenged world leaders to remember
who would inherit the results of their decisions.

more than enough, we are afraid to share. We are afraid to let go of some of our wealth.

"In Canada, we live the privileged life, with plenty of food, water, and shelter—we have watches, bicycles, computers, and television sets. The list could go on for two days.

"Two days ago here in Brazil, we were shocked when we spent time with some children living on the streets. This is what one child told us. 'I wish I was rich and if I were, I would give all the street children food, clothes, medicines, shelter, and love and affection.' If a child on the streets who has nothing, is willing to share, why are we who have everything still so greedy? I can't stop thinking that these are children my own age, that it makes a tremendous difference where you are born, that I could be one of those children living in the favelas of Rio; I could be a child starving in Somalia; or a victim of war in the Middle East; or a beggar in India.

"I am only a child, yet I know if all the money spent on war was spent on finding environmental answers, ending poverty, and finding treaties, what a wonderful place this earth would be!"

A camera panned the room where the girl was speaking, focussing on delegates watching solemn and unsmiling. Many eyes glistened with tears.

"At school, even in kindergarten, you teach us how to behave in the world. You teach us not to fight with others, to work things out, to respect others, to clean up our mess, not to hurt other creatures, to share—not be greedy. Then why do you go out and do the things you tell us not to do? Do not forget why you are attending these conferences, who you are doing this for—we are your own children.

"You are deciding what kind of a world we are growing up in. Parents should be able to comfort their children by saying everything's going to be all right, it's not the end of the world, and we're doing the best we can. But I don't think you can say that to us anymore. Are we even on your list of priorities?

"My dad always says, 'You are what you do, not what you say.' Well, what you do makes me cry at night. You grown-ups say you love us. But I challenge you, please make your actions reflect your words.

"Thank you."

From the plenary hall to the conference corridors outside, applause erupted. The delegates jumped to their feet for an ovation.

The delegates were still standing and clapping as Severn walked off the stage. It was all a blur. Inside she was still enveloped in the intensity behind her words—the deep anger and sadness with which she challenged the world's leaders.

Severn reached her parents. "Mommy could you hear my heart beating?"

Michelle, Vanessa, and Morgan tackled her with a group hug. Severn imagined Tove was with them. It seemed like a dream—but the crazy dream had come true. "We did it!"

"Congratulations!" said a man, thrusting his hand toward her.

At first, she didn't recognize the man she had last seen in jeans at the Earth Parliament. Then her dad whispered, "That's Al Gore—a real good guy."

The Senator clasped her hand gently. "That was the best speech anyone has given here in Rio!"

From left, Vanessa, Michelle, Morgan, and
Sarika congratulate Severn on her speech.

Raffi was also on hand to help celebrate.

Epilogue

"We know there are a lot more kids like us out there. The next step is to join together. The more of us that work together, the more we can accomplish. It is up to us. It is our planet and our future."

Vanessa Suttie, Morgan Geisler, Michelle Quigg,

Severn Cullis-Suzuki, and Tove Fenger

While the ECO girls were enjoying a wonderful adventure in the Ariau Jungle Towers, Maurice Strong, Secretary-General of the United Nations Conference on Environment and Development, gave the following remarks in his closing speech:

"Mr. President, Distinguished Delegates,

"I think you all will agree that we must change the course that we have been on...the voices of the children we heard here as our session closed all tell us why we are doing it—we're doing it for them. They have a right to expect it from us; they are going to hold us accountable for what we do after Rio, about the decisions you have taken here.

"You heard from a fellow Canadian, a lovely young twelve-year-old girl, Severn Cullis-Suzuki. And I want to close these remarks, Mr. President, by reminding you of what she said, which I believe every child on this planet will have in his or her heart as they look at what you have done here at Rio.

"She said, 'Parents used to be able to comfort their children by saying everything's going to be all right...but, you can't say

Michelle, Morgan, Severn, Sarika, and Vanessa
finally got to visit the rainforest near Manaus, Brazil.

that to us anymore. Our planet is becoming worse and worse for all future children. Yet we only hear adults talking about local interests and national priorities. Are we even on your list of priorities? You grown-ups say you love us, but we challenge you to make your actions reflect your words.'

"We are all challenged, Mr. President, in the responsibilities we carry as we leave Rio, to make our actions reflect the words which have testified to our commitment here.

"Thank you, Mr. President."

Delegates considered the 1992 Earth Summit a success. They signed declarations to combat climate change and preserve bio-diversity. Canada called on all nations to adopt an Earth Charter of Rights and Responsibilities. Never before had there been a common commitment from so many countries—179—to sign the action plan Agenda 21, a wish-list for a global sustainable twenty-first century where people's needs are met in the present without compromising the needs of future generations. Agenda 21 also included a chapter to give children and youth a voice as partners in decision-making. This led to the United Nations Tunza Youth Strategy, which elects a youth board to the United Nations Environmental Program (UNEP).

Today, youth all over the world are continuing to stand up and speak out for environmental, social, and intergenerational justice. They still want adults to listen and to change their ways.

Michelle, Vanessa, Sarika, Morgan, and Severn were tired, but happy with their efforts and the impact they had made at the Rio Summit.

Glossary

Activist: Someone who is involved in actions to bring about change—social, political, environmental, or other change.

Advocate: To speak, write, and argue in support of a particular cause or issue.

Agenda 21: A global action plan to encourage cooperation among nations for sustaining life on Earth while growing equitable economies. It was voluntarily adopted by 179 governments at the UN Earth Summit in 1992.

Biodiversity: All the plants and animals that exist in the natural world.

Clear-cut logging: A method that cuts down all the trees.

Climate change/Global warming: Climate change refers to general changes in temperature, precipitation, winds, and other climate patterns. Global warming refers to the general rise in surface temperature of Earth. Pollution and the use of fossil fuels and are causing the changes.

Colonialism: The control and exploitation by a stronger country of weaker one; the conquered territories are called colonies.

Developing country: A country that is poor and whose citizens are mostly agricultural workers, but one that aspires to become more advanced socially and economically. Also known as a Third World nation.

Extinction: The disappearance of a species or group of species forever.

Haida Gwaii: An archipelago of 138 islands (formerly the Queen Charlotte Islands).

Glossary

Indigenous peoples: The original settlers of continents, who have lived in the same region for centuries or millennia.

Intergenerational justice: The concept of fairness between generations. The unsustainable use of natural resources today, leads to injustice for the following generations.

Manioc: A long, woody root with soft brittle stems that is a starchy staple in the Kayapo diet. It is also known as cassava and yucca.

Non-governmental organization (NGO): An organization that is privately funded (mostly by donations from the general public) and is independent from government policy.

Old-growth forests: A mature ecosystem that hasn't changed much over time or been influenced by human activity, and exhibits unique ecological features.

Overpopulation: A population that grows so large or dense that it causes depletion of resources, environmental deterioration, and the prevalence of famine and disease.

Plenary Session: An important meeting at a conference that everyone is expected to attend.

Rainforest: A forest with a heavy annual rainfall.

Regalia: Traditional ceremonial dress of indigenous peoples.

Severn Bore: When the conditions are right, the incoming tide meets the water at the mouth of the Severn River to create a large surge wave—the second highest tidal range in the world (up to 50 feet or 15.4m).

Sustainability: Human activity should be guided by the principle that the needs of the present generation should not harm the ability of future generations to meet their needs.

Tunza: An African word meaning to treat with care and affection.

United Nations: A collection of countries working together for peace. It was founded in 1945 after World War II to prevent wars between countries.

Useful Links

Severn's speech in Rio '92:
http://www.janetwilson.ca/severn-and-the-day-she-silenced-the-world.html

CBC video of ECO made at the Earth Summit, 1992:
http://www.youtube.com/watch?v=JYEqS10HlwA

Earth Charter:
http://www.earthcharterinaction.org

United Nations Environmental Programme:
http://www.unep.org

TUNZA:
http://www.unep.org/tunza/ or http://tunza.eco-generation.org

Girls Action Foundation:
http://girlsactionfoundation.ca

The David Suzuki Foundation:
http://www.davidsuzuki.org

Children's Eternal Rainforest:
http://friendsoftherainforest.org/

Rainforest Action Network:
http://ran.org

World Council of Indigenous Peoples:
http://wcip2014.org

http://www.ecokids.ca

http://www.earthday.ca

Severn Says

When I gave the speech in Rio, I had no idea the UN had taped it until we received a video. My mom made copies and sent it out to people who requested it. Years later the Internet was invented. Then "The Girl who Silenced the World for Six Minutes" appeared on YouTube. I still can't believe it has been viewed many millions of times and it remains relevant and poignant even today.

After Rio, my ECO friends went to different high schools. I played basketball. I enjoyed science. The following year, I received the UN Environment Program's Global 500 Award in Beijing. I continued to give inspirational speeches at other large environmental conferences around the world, including the 1997 and 2002 UN World Summits, where I was on the UN Special Advisory Panel. My activism included a cross-Canada cycling campaign to raise awareness about climate change and air pollution. I helped develop a youth think-tank. I went to Yale University in the U.S. for my degree in Ecology and Evolutionary Biology and to the University of Victoria in British Columbia where I studied Ethnoecology with Kwakwaka'wakw elders. I

Severn returned to Aucre in 2001 as a university student.

also published several books, co-hosted the TV series *Suzuki's Nature Quest* and *Samaqan—Water Stories*. I'm very proud of my work on the Earth Charter, a code of values for our conduct toward the planet. All of these amazing things happened because I followed my passion for the Earth.

In the years since I addressed the world leaders and asked them to remember their children when they made decisions, I've committed my life to advocate for intergenerational justice, long-term sustainability, and awareness of the interconnection between culture and environment. But those few minutes that I spoke remain the most powerful action I have ever taken. I've grown up, but people are still talking about that speech. Why? Well, I think it is because people really need to hear from children who can see and speak the truth in a way like nobody else can.

As I look back over how little action has been taken by world leaders since Rio '92, it would be easy to be discouraged and lose hope. But today I am a parent. I have two little boys. Now, I'm not only fighting for my future—I'm fighting for the future of my kids. I will do everything I can to make sure that they have great opportunities. Love—love for the Earth, and especially love for our children—is the most powerful force we have for change.

—Severn Cullis-Suzuki, Haida Gwaii, 2013

ECO KIDS:
The world in their

It's written all over their faces – youthful energy and a commitment to the environment. These are the five winners of the VanCity Youth Environmental Service Award.

Morgan Geisler, Vanessa Suttie, Severn Cullis-Suzuki, Tove Fenger and Michelle Quigg are collectively known as the "Eco Kids."

As members of the Environmental Children's Organization, they began working together two years ago when they were all students at Lord Tennyson school in Vancouver.

With imaginative fund-raising (they made and sold Eco Gecko lizard brooches) they made enough money to buy a water filter for a Penan village in Sarawak.

Later, they held a special night at the Vancouver Planetarium that raised enough money to send them to the Earth Summit in Brazil. There they met with delegates and diplomats and put forward a children's perspective on the environment.

VanCity helped finance Eco Kids newspaper and was active in helping raise funds for their trip to Brazil.

The ECO girls after winning the VanCity Youth Environmental Service Award.

Where Are They Now?

Two weeks after Rio, Senator Al Gore was chosen to be the vice-presidential running mate to Bill Clinton, who became the next President of the United States. He recommended the establishment of a "Mission to Planet Earth," a plan for children to staff a worldwide monitoring system to rescue the planet. He wrote a book and made a film, *An Inconvenient Truth*, warning the world about climate change.

Paiakan and the Kayapo have lost their fight to save their land from the Belo Monte Dam complex—the third largest in the world. Eighty percent of the Xingu River's flow will be

Tara and David

Sarika

diverted, devastating an area of more than 580 square miles (1,500 sq km) of Brazilian rainforest, creating the largest man-made lake in the world and displacing between 20,000 and 40,000 people. Baby Majal is studying to be an indigenous rights lawyer. The Penan are also still struggling to save their land.

David Suzuki, Tara Cullis, Doug Tompkins, Jeff Gibbs, Doug Ragan, and Raffi continue to be passionate environmental activists. Sarika Cullis-Suzuki has earned her PhD in Marine Biology and is still interested in the ocean and fish, and the conservation of biodiversity. She is a member of the World Wildlife Fund's Canada Oceans Advisory Committee, and a board member of the David Suzuki Foundation.

The Golden Toad, discovered by young Jerry James in Costa Rica, is now extinct. Scientists blame the increasing levels of ultraviolet radiation entering the Earth's atmosphere due to ozone depletion.

Tove Fenger's experience with ECO influenced her more than she thought it would. In high school, she participated in another youth organization: Leadership Initiative For Earth, which fostered youth leadership on environmental issues. Tove believes that working with both of these groups led her toward a path in the public service. She now works in British Columbia's Department of Aboriginal Affairs.

Tove

Morgan Geisler (now Westcott) is General Manager of an organization called LinkBC —the tourism education network. Her job includes helping tourism students across British Columbia find work in the hospitality industry. She runs

Morgan and her family

Michelle

Vanessa

a sustainability competition called Project Change, encouraging BC's tourism, adventure, and hospitality students to make a difference in their communities. Morgan lives in East Vancouver with her husband and daughter.

Michelle Quigg lives in Vancouver with her husband and two children. She works as a lawyer for a non-profit organization connecting people of limited means with lawyers willing to volunteer their services. Social justice and love of Nature remain core values in her life.

Vanessa Suttie (now Cybulski) was profoundly changed by joining ECO. It was the first time she had worked in a group with others of like mind and realized she had a voice and that people listened. Her first experience of witnessing poverty in the developing world also shaped the woman she became—caring of her neighbors, her community, and the world around her. Presently she is busy with the most important task of all—motherhood. Vanessa lives in Vancouver with her husband and two children.

Severn Cullis-Suzuki lives on Haida Gwaii with her husband and two children. She is a board member of the Haida Gwaii Higher Education Society, the David Suzuki Foundation, and Spark—Girls Action Foundation. She is studying the Haida language. She hopes her pursuit of traditional and scientific knowledge and her dedication to using her voice will help promote a culture of diversity, sustainability, and joy. Severn continues to inspire the youth of each new generation to believe they have an important part to play in reminding adults what is at stake and to stand up and speak out for social, intergenerational, and environmental justice.

Severn and her family

Photo Credits

Cover: Jeff Topham (top), Cullis-Suzuki family (bottom)
Cullis-Suzuki family: pages vii, 2, 6, 7, 12, 16, 21, 22, 26, 27, 35, 41, 45, 46, 50 (bottom), 52, 80, 84, 134, 171, 173, 178, 182 (below), 186, 202, 208
Jeff Gibbs, www.jeffgibbs.org: 14, 15, 34, 63, 64, 69
©Cristina Mittermeier: 28, 33, 37, 40, 50 (top)
Michelle Quigg: 108, 119, 126, 132, 135, 150, 160, 162, 166, 200
Morgan Geisler: 113, 120, 127, 129, 130, 141, 142, 151, 156, 157, 158, 164, 182 (top), 199
Vanessa Suttie: 78, 96, 137, 165, 184, 200
ECO Newsletter: 88, 93, 99, 100, 102, 114
Tove Fenger: 95

Rod Burns, www.boldpoint348.wordpress.com: 5

Bradley Davis, BackpackPhotography: 9

Michiko Sakata: 18

Jon Rawlinson, www.jonrawlinson.com: 40

Bjørn Christian Tørrissen, www.bjornfree.com: 42

US fish and wildlife services: 57 (top)

Thom Henley, www.thomhenley.com: 74

Friends of the Children's Eternal Rainforest: 56, 57 (bottom)

Nicole Roy Leonard: 86

UN Photo/Claudio Edinger: 116

Raffi Cavoukian, www.childhonouring.org: 106

Jeff Topham, www.jefftopham.com: 194

The Vancouver Sun: 196

The David Suzuki Foundation: 198

John Badcock: 198 (bottom)

Linda Johnston: 207

* Please note: Some photos listed here may not have been taken by the people who kindly supplied them.

Acknowledgments

Writers of true stories depend on the goodwill and cooperation of the people they write about. This book could never have been published without the help and approval of the main characters, Severn, Michelle, Morgan, Tove, and Vanessa. I am very grateful for their patience and grace in answering all my many pesky and personal questions. Thanks to Raffi and to the ECO parents who agreed to be interviewed and helped in many ways. I especially appreciate the generosity of Severn and her family for permitting me to research their precious story and write it in the form of creative non-fiction.

Information was taken from several books: *David Suzuki, The Autobiography*, Greystone Books, 2006; *Raffi, The Life of a Children's Troubadour, an autobiography*, Homeland Press, 2000;

Tell the World, A Young Environmentalist Speaks Out, by Severn Cullis-Suzuki, Doubleday Canada, 1993; *Notes from Canada's Young Activists,* Greystone Books, 2007; *Rescue Mission Planet Earth: A children's edition of Agenda 21,* Kingfisher Books, 1994.

My heartfelt thanks go to the following people: Morgan Geisler who trusted me with her wonderful personal diary; Michelle Quigg for sending me ECO newsletters; everyone who took the time to read through drafts, especially Yasemin Ucar, Linda Sword, and Ed Langevin; my husband, Chris Wilson, who processed the newsletter and diary images, and helped in many ways. I appreciate everyone who provided photos, especially B.C. photographers Jeff Gibbs and Jeff Topham, and photographer Cristina Mittermeier who generously donated the use of the Kayapo images to raise awareness and support for the rights of the Kayapo and all indigenous peoples. Kudos to the staff at Second Story Press—to my editors Carolyn Jackson and Kelly Jones, to Margie Wolfe who recognizes and supports good and important stories, to Melissa Kaita in production, Phuong Truong the general manager, and Emma Rodgers in marketing and publicity. I thank the Ontario Arts Council Writers' Reserve for their support.

About the Author

Janet Wilson is an author and fine artist. She is the writer and illustrator of *Our Rights: How Kids are Changing the World*, *Our Earth: How Kids are Saving the Planet*, and *One Peace: True Stories of Young Activists*. Her great admiration for young people inspired her to write *Shannen and the Dream for a School*, about Shannen Koostachin's fight for a new school for the First Nations community of Attawapiskat. Janet lives in Eden Mills, Ontario, a community with a strong environmental focus.